Interesting Characte

By

David Scholey

The cover picture is a painting of the 1820 era Flesh Market in Newcastle by James Richardson, a good friend of mine, more details of Jim's work can be found at http://james-richardson.artistwebsites.com

And at www.janpa-arts.co.uk

James is the 1st cousin 5 times removed of Thomas Miles Richardson senior who appears in the final chapter of this book and the sketch is based on the original 1820 sketch by Thomas Miles Richardson senior

© 2019 David Scholey

Interesting Characters of the North East

In this edition I have tried to bring to life some of the characters of the North East who have helped to mould our lives and our memories.

Invariably some of the more well-known characters have made their way to the pages, Hotspur for instance is well written about already but not so many people know the story of Roger Thornton who is one of his close neighbours high above Northumberland Street.

I have tried to bring to life the original "Dirty Dick" the famous chemist on Clayton Street until the 1970s

Here too is the inventor of Be-Ro Flour and the inventor of plasticine.

The story behind the famous Wooden Dollies of North Shields is also here.

Much has been written about the famous artist from Haydon Bridge John Martin, but less is generally known about his brothers Jonathan who set fire to York Minster or William Martin who invented and sold for £5 the perpetual motion machine. Few people too, know about the tragic killing of their sister.

Joseph Swan is well known for his part in the invention of the light bulb but how many know how he fitted in with the bookseller Mawson Swan & Morgan or the chemist Mawson & Proctor.

The artistic family The Richardsons also feature in the following pages

I hope that you enjoy reading this book and I will welcome feedback

David Scholey

February 2019

david_scholey@yahoo.com

Interesting Characters of the North East

Contents

Dirty Dick's the Chemist

Statues of Northumberland Street

      Thomas Bewick

      Sir Henry Percy (Hotspur)

      Sir John Marlay

      Roger Thornton

The Mad Martins of Haydon Bridge

      William Martin

      Jonathan Martin

      Richard Martin

      Ann Martin

      John Martin

Thomas Bell & Be-Ro Flour

Plasticine & North Shields

The Wooden Dollies of North Shields

Mawson Swan & Morgan

The Artistic Richardsons

Dirty Dicks the Chemist

Dirty Dicks was a chemist's shop in Newcastle upon Tyne known and loved by thousands until it closed in the early 1970's.

Rather than allow history to erase it I felt a few words about it would help it to remain on record.

It was a unique chemist shop in the 20th century. People went to it because traditional doctors had failed to cure the ailment and there was a certain confidence that Dirty Dick would succeed where medical practitioners had failed.

In 1970 I myself went, I had suffered shingles for nearly a year and it didn't matter what treatment my GP prescribed nothing worked.

The appearance of the shop itself was hardly inspiring of confidence.

It was a tradition that the shutters remained in place even when open. It stood at 105 Clayton Street Newcastle next door to Woolworth. Inside, the shop was equally drab, the shelves stacked high with bottles the size shape and colour would have been familiar to Dickens.

There was invariably a queue, some knew exactly what they wanted, I was one of those who required an examination and advice.

When my turn came the chemist took me into his examination room and I took off my shirt to show my shoulder a mass of red weal's and scabs, despite my best efforts I was constantly scratching in an effort to ease the incessant pain.

His examination took barely thirty seconds, soon I was dressed and in the main shop waiting for him to finish creating a remedy.

It was a thick almost grey paste. Cautiously I applied it as instructed twice a day,

Within a week he achieved what no doctor had been able to the pain and itch were gone and my shoulder was starting to revert to normal.

That was my personal experience of Dirty Dick and I know with certainty that thousands more can attest to the successes of that grim looking shop.

So, who? Why? How?

Well a chemist had stood at 105 Clayton Street since the 1840s however there were at least five other chemists operating on Clayton street alone let alone other parts of Newcastle so why was this one so successful?

At first it wasn't, Wards Directory in 1865 show that the shop was named T Herring

Another year it was Francis Marshall

In 1867 it became J Crozier and that is where Dirty Dick began. James Crozer or Crozier, the records do vary, was a unique chemist.

Let's look firstly at what a 19th century chemist actually was:

The nineteenth century saw not only the survival of traditional fringe practitioners-folk healers, wise-women, midwives, bone-setters, and itinerant quacks-but also the flourishing of new unorthodox and para-medical groups, including homeopathists, hydropathic practitioners, medical botanists, and chemists and druggists. By the mid-nineteenth century, chemists and druggists made up the most numerous group of para-medical personnel

While the most clearly-defined function of the nineteenth century chemist and druggist was to make up the prescriptions of qualified medical men, this was not normally their most important function, and they also engaged themselves in a number of what can be described as medical or even fringe activities. These activities, which included "over-the-counter-prescribing", the making up of family recipes, and the sale of a wide range of drugs and patent remedies, accounted for the largest proportion of the chemist and druggist's trade.

Since 1841 attempts had been made to regulate the activities of pharmacist's chemists and druggist with no real success. The 1868 Pharmacy Act strove to confine 15 poisons to be available only to registered pharmacists but the wording of the act was so vague that it was wide open to abuse.

Now let's look at James Crozier; who he was and how he came to be a chemist at all.

To discover him properly let's go even farther back in time to an earlier James Crozier in Roxburghshire Scotland, born in 1667 he married Marion Lyden who was 7 years older than him.

On 3rd April 1687 they had a son George Crozier, like his father he would work the land and in due course he went on to marry Margaret Beattie

This couple were quite old when their son, another James was born in 1740, he too married a member of the Beattie family; Christian Beattie.

On 24th December 1769 another James was born to James and Christian

This James married Jane Hogg in 1795 in Cornhill-on-Tweed, she claimed a relationship to Captain Cook, I have not been able to prove or disprove this but their eldest son was certainly named William Cook Crozier. Another son was, predictably called James

There were in fact six children at least: Margaret born 1799, Jane born 1803 William Cook born 1812 James born 1813, Eleanor date of birth unknown and John date of birth unknown.

James senior was to say the least quite a character, he operated a nurseryman business in Alnwick and Newcastle under the style J Crozier and Co, by all accounts he was a superb horticulturist and numerous newspaper accounts attest to this, there was however another side to him. For a while he was employed by Newcastle Infirmary to attend to the gardens there. For some reason he was dismissed from this post.

The matron was then accused of keeping 50 ducks on the grounds for her own benefit in other words that she was rearing them for food for herself and not for the patients.

The accusation came from James Crozier.

A subsequent investigation found that not a single duck could be found anywhere on the grounds of the hospital.

He appeared as a witness in a court case Snowdens v Hartley involving an alkali company disposing of waste and so damaging vegetation, despite his evidence not being accepted by the jury he wrote angry letters to the papers insisting his view was correct. Indeed, there was a large volume of correspondence on the matter after the court had already decided against Hartley's.

He became a Freemason on May 9th 1803 in the Alnwick Lodge.

In 1828 he issued a notice refusing to be liable for any debts incurred by his wife or any of his children.

In 1832 his son John ostensibly took over the business, however James seems to have retained actual control. A reason for the change of ownership can be conjectured by the fact that he became a bankrupt in 1836. One has to assume he had been pursued on various occasions by creditors in the last few years and had been trying to stay a step ahead of them.

He made various inventions each of which was in his words astonishing, one was a device for watering turnips.

His wife Jane died on 7th May 1833 and he seems then to have set up home in Wallsend.

Most remarkably this man was involved with none other than the architect John Dobson in the creation of Brandling Villas

Jesmond, Newcastle upon Tyne It is not clear what his actual role was but he was one of three individuals including Dobson to whom any enquiries should be addressed. It seems that in fact he did own one of the properties Jessamine Cottage which stood just north of Brandling Place.

It is his son however who was responsible for the lasting fame of Dirty Dicks.

Being the son of a nurseryman, it can be assumed initially that he will have been aware of many of the values of certain herbs from a medical point of view.

He initially served his chemist apprenticeship in Berwick and later worked for a Mr Garbutt of Gateshead chemist. He made the acquaintance of a Dr White who arranged a job for him in America as a dispensing chemist.

From there he visited Cuba, Jamaica and other parts of the West Indies.

Subsequent to that he travelled to India, China and Hong Kong in these places he worked as a dispenser in various hospitals.

From these roles he then began serving as surgeon aboard various vessels operating between Shanghai and the Indian Ocean and the Rajah which was a passenger ship operating between England and Australia.

One must assume that this global hopping will have made him aware of various herbal and differing medical treatments around the world, I suspect that this experience played a vital role in the success of Dirty Dicks

He returned to England in around about 1866 as Wards directory shows him as the proprietor of the business from 1867.

Prior to his ownership there had long been an apothecary shop on the site. In 1840 E Marshall took the business on. He was followed by a Mr Barkas in partnership with Dr Pearse. In 1860 Mr Thomas Heron took the business on.

He then sold the shop at 105 Clayton Street to James Crozer for £68 paid as a fifty-pound note and £18 in gold.

James Crozer was tall gaunt and unkempt, so unkempt that his appearance gave the shop its lasting nickname. It seems that he was as eccentric as his father

Frugality was his lifestyle, he ate at Lockhart's café on hot water and a penny's-worth of rice.

One day while at lunch the shop was broken into and the safe rifled. This caused him to always leave the shutters up, in turn this helped make the shop readily obvious to customers.

Apparently, he never cleaned the shop, it was full of cobwebs, the rows of old bottles and jars were thick with dust and the shop was lit with oil lamps and candles.

In 1881 before his retirement he lived at 15 Stowell Street, along with him lived his 82-year-old sister Margaret, an Irish born housekeeper Maria Frank aged 29, her daughter Mary aged 6 and a lodger from Surrey, John Curry a travelling salesman.

He retired from business in about 1887 having sold it to J H Forster which became ltd company in 1914.

In 1937 Alan M Todd joined the company as an assistant and by 1972 was the managing director.

He was finding it harder and harder to locate the medical compounds which had been used in the shop's history and this together with the massive costs when he could locate them coupled with his own advancing years forced him to close the company down.

Even if the materials had been more readily available training a successor to continue running the shop in the time-honoured manner would have been long and arduous.

There was only one assistant at the time and they went to work for Mawson & Proctor who for a while supplied ongoing treatment to old patrons of Dirty Dick.

As for Dirty Dick himself; James Crozer he died on 16th June 1888 at his final home the earlier mentioned 1 Jessamine Cottage Brandling Village.

In his will he left £4084 5s 6d approximately £350,000 in modern money. It was left to his sister Margaret, his sister Eleanor now Eleanor Gray and his brother William Cook Crozer.

He is buried in Westgate Hill Cemetery.

Statues of Northumberland Street

When walking north on Northumberland Street it will be easy to miss the memorial to four memorable individuals of Newcastle's past. In order to spot them, when, having passed Fenwick's walking towards the Haymarket gaze your eye up to the next building numbered 45 Northumberland Street. It may be easier from the opposite side of the road.

You will see 4 figures beautifully carved out on the stonework

The statues are in tribute to four heroes of the area, Thomas Bewick, Harry Hotspur. John Marley and Roger Thornton

The building until 1977 had been the home of Boots the Chemist, they had acquired it following a take over in around 1911 of J. H. Inman. When under the ownership of Inman's, the front of the shop at ground level was as seen below. This was the first venture into the north east of what was then called Boots Cash Chemist and a specific company was created to handle the area Boots Cash Chemists (Northern).

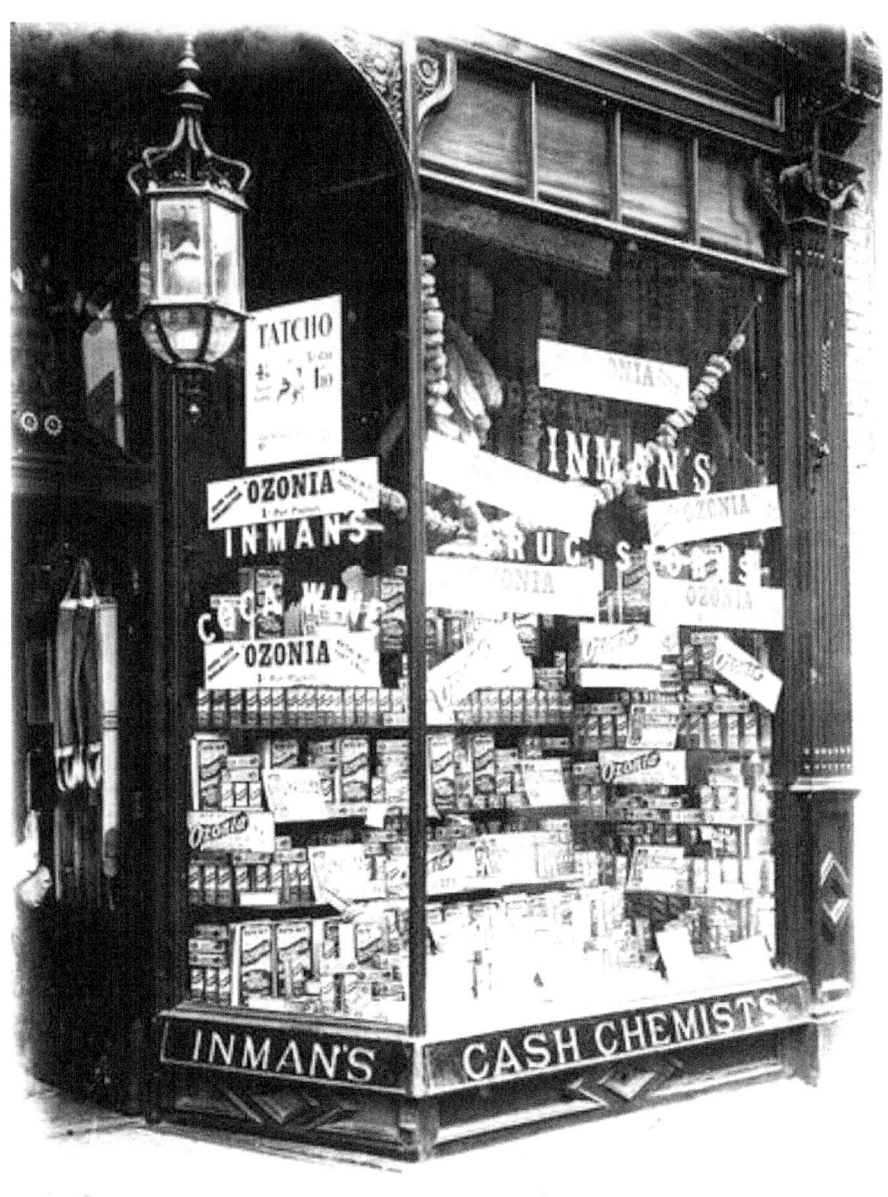

The frontage of the old Inman's Chemist

At the time it was usual for Boots to have similarly designed frontage to their shops and generally the designer would have been Morley Horder. However most of his work was in the 1920s. In this case the plans for the work were submitted to

Newcastle Council on 30th October 1912 by M V Treleaven who was the architect and surveyor for Boots at that time

Thomas Bewick

As regards the statues themselves, the first or upper left is that of **Thomas Bewick**.

Bewick was born in Cherryburn in the village of Mickley near Stocksfield in Northumberland. His exact birthdate is a matter of conjecture as it was either 10th or 11th August 1753 but for some reason he celebrated it on the 12th.

He was born the eldest child of John Bewick and John's second wife Jane Wilson (his first wife had been Ann Toppin). John was a tenant farmer who also rented a small colliery at Mickley Bank and employed six men.

Thomas attended school at Ovingham where is on record as being a poor scholar however he did excel at drawing.

When he was 14 he was apprenticed to Ralph Beilby, a Newcastle engraver, it was there that he learnt the likes of jewellery and cutlery with coats of arms and family names.

He also learnt to engrave on wood and in time that became his passion and developed the use of metal engraving tools to be used on hard boxwood across the grain. The result was high quality illustrations at a lower price.

In 1776 at 23 years old he became a partner in the business and in time the business acquired the reputation of being Newcastle's leading engraving service.

Ten years later he married Isabella Elliott from Ovingham, his childhood sweetheart.

He is described as being of athletic build standing 6 feet tall, he is on record as being brave and not scared of standing up to bullies.

He also had strict morals and was fiercely opposed to animal cruelty taking up issues such as the docking of horses' tails, performing animals and cruelty to dogs. He was also opposed to war.

In 1790 Bewick and Beilby published "The History of Quadrupeds".

This inspired the two to prepare the "History of British Birds" the

first volume was to be "Land Birds".

THE YELLOW OWL,

GILLIHOWLET, CHURCH, BARN, OR SCREECH OWL.

(*Strix flammea*, Linn.—*Chouette effraie*, Temm.)

Bewick prepared the illustrations and Beilby was supposed to provide the text but struggled to do so. This was the beginning of their falling out. Bewick had to write most of the text and refused to allow Beilby to be named as co-author.

A paragraph was added at the end of the book explaining:

"*It may be proper to observe, that while one of the editors of this work was engaged in preparing the Engravings, the compilation of the descriptions was undertaken by the other, subject, however, to the corrections of his friend, whose habits led him to a more intimate acquaintance with this branch of Natural History. – Land Birds, Preface.*"

The book proved highly successful when published by Beilby and Bewick in 1797 and, after completing another on "Kings and Queens of England" Bewick was keen to commence the second volume "Water Birds"

The earlier dispute about authorship arose again and that brought about the break-up of the partnership.

It cost Bewick £20 in legal fees and £21 for his share of the workshop (in modern terms multiply these figures by around 100!)

Water Birds was published with the help of his apprentices in 1804

THE HERON.

COMMON HERON, HERONSEWGH, OR HERONSHAW.

(*Ardea Cinerea*, Lath.—*Héron cendré*, Temm.)

He became a celebrity in his own lifetime and died 8th November 1828 at home and is buried in Ovingham churchyard next to Isabella who had died two years earlier.

There is a bust of him at the site of his workshop in St Nicholas churchyard Newcastle

Sir Henry Percy (Harry Hotspur)

The next statue is that of Harry Hotspur or to be more precise **Sir Henry Percy**

Henry Percy was born 20 May 1364 probably at Alnwick Castle in Northumberland.) He was the eldest son of Henry Percy, 1st Earl of Northumberland, and Margaret Neville, who was the daughter of Ralph de Neville, 2nd Lord Neville of Raby, and Alice de Audley.

His name was made virtually immortal by Shakespeare. Using both names Percy and Hotspur he appears in Henry IV Part 1.

Shakespeare does however use some poetic licence by painting him as a contemporary of Prince "Hal" the future King Henry V. In reality Hotspur was 23 years older than Prince Hal.

He did begin his active life at a very young age. In April 1377, at not quite 13 years old he was knighted by Edward III.

By 1385 he was battling the Scots and it was they who gave him his nickname Hotspur. It came about due to how reckless he was in instigating an attack. (Hot to the Spur) The actual name in Scottish vernacular was Haatspore.

HE then represented the King fighting in France and was made a Knight of the Garter.

He was sent on a diplomatic mission to Cyprus in June 1393 and appointed Governor of Bordeaux, deputy to John of Gaunt, 1st Duke of Lancaster in the Duchy of Aquitane.

The King at this time was Richard II. However, when Henry Bolingbroke led a rebellion against King Richard, Percy and his father supported Bolingbroke and marched south with the rebel forces from Doncaster.

Bolingbroke became King Henry IV and the two Percy's were lavishly rewarded for their part.

Hotspur among other things was made High Sheriff of Flintshire and later Royal Lieutenant of North Wales.

Despite the honours Hotspur became increasingly unhappy with Henry IV, he had failed to pay him for defending the Scottish Border, the King demanded that Scottish prisoners were handed over to him, he failed to give proper support in Wales and even put his own son in Wales over him. The final straw was the King's failure to ransom Hotspurs brother in law Sir Edmund Mortimer who had been captured by the Welsh in 1402.

This led to Hotspur denouncing what he called the Kings tyrannical government.

Their anger with the King grew so that in the summer of 1403 they rose up and took arms against the King. It is likely that they were already in collusion with Owen Glendower (Glyndwr) the last native Welshman to hold the title of Prince of Wales.

Hotspur together with his uncle Thomas Percy the Earl of Worcester marched to Shrewsbury arriving on 21st July 1403, his fathers' troops had been delayed so without that additional force Hotspur and Worcester began battle with the King's troops. When Hotspur was killed in that battle the troops fled.

Legend states that he was killed by an arrow in the face when he opened his visor for a better view. Two days later his uncle was executed.

King Henry is reported to have wept when he saw Hotspur's body and later when legends circulated that in Fact Hotspur was still alive the King had his body exhumed and displayed in the Market Place of Shrewsbury. His head was then taken to York and impaled on Micklegate Bar and the rest of his body divided and taken to London, Newcastle upon Tyne, Bristol and Chester before being given to his widow Elizabeth who had the remains buried in York Minster. He was declared a traitor and his lands seized by the Crown.

His wife mentioned above was Elizabeth Mortimer the eldest child of Edmund Mortimer the Earl of March and his wife Philippa the daughter of the 1st Duke of Clarence.

They had two children: Henry 1393-1455 who married Eleanor Neville he was killed at the Battle of St Albans during the War of the Roses and Elizabeth who married twice firstly to Baron John Clifford and on his death to Ralph Neville, Earl of Westmorland

As recently as 2010 a 14-foot statue of Hotspur was unveiled by the Duke of Northumberland in Alnwick, close to the castle.

Sir John Marlay

Sir John Marley or Marlay (1590–1673) was an English merchant, military commander and politician of the seventeenth century. He is best remembered for his heroic defence of Newcastle-upon-Tyne during the English Civil War, when he held the town for seven months against a besieging army on behalf of the Royalist cause. Out of poverty and desperation he later betrayed the cause he had served so loyally, and as a result to the end of his life he was reviled by many of his former friends as a traitor.

His name is commemorated by Marlay House and Marlay Park near Dublin city, which were built by his descendants, who settled in Ireland.

He was the son of William Marley: his father was a Hostman and a Merchant Adventurer in Newcastle upon Tyne. John became an alehouse keeper and then a colliery owner, Hostman & Merchant Adventurer: the latter occupation brought him great wealth, with an estimated income of £4500 a year, and he ran a victualling business as well. He was prominent in local Government from the late 1630s: he was three times Mayor of Newcastle-upon-Tyne, his native town, and represented that constituency in the House of Commons from 1661 until his death. He was knighted in 1639. He obtained the victualling contract for the English Army during the First Bishops' War.

Siege of Newcastle

During the English Civil War, he was appointed by King Charles I as military Governor of Newcastle-upon-Tyne, as well as being its Mayor 1642–44, and he defended the town with great spirit during the lengthy siege of 1644. He held off the besieging Scots army for seven months, and on 17 October he refused to surrender the town even after the Scots army had mined the walls. When the town was stormed on 19 October, he and the garrison fought their way from street to street, then retreated into the Castle. He held out there for another three days, and then surrendered on the promise of mercy for himself and his men. However, Hodgson has the siege lasting from 13 August to 20 October. Charleton concurs as to the start and has the town in possession by the Scots on 19 October with Sir John and his officers retreating to the Castle keep for four days. With him were several Scots lords including Ludovic Lindsay, 16th Earl of Crawford, Robert Maxwell, 1st Earl of Nithsdale, and Lord Reed, together with their fellow Royalists Sir Nicholas Cole, 1st Baronet of Brancepeth Castle, Sir George Baker and the clergyman Dr. George Wishart, later Bishop of Edinburgh.

Exile and treason

The promise of mercy was kept, but the Royalist leaders did not escape punishment entirely. Lord Crawford was threatened with the death penalty, although it was not carried out, and Dr. Wishart was imprisoned for a time. For the offence of having refused the terms of surrender, Marlay was proscribed, banished and driven into exile: he lived mainly in the Spanish Netherlands. Parliament forfeited his estates, and sold his collieries, and he sank into wretched poverty. He was reduced to such desperate straits that in 1658 he offered to sell to Oliver Cromwell all Royalist plans for the restoration of Charles II, in return for £100 and permission to return home, although he insisted, rather ludicrously, that "he would do nothing underhand". His reputation never recovered from this betrayal: John Thurloe, Cromwell's spymaster, thought that it was a terrible blow to the Royalist cause. Marley returned to England, but the Government ignored his pleas for money, and he was clearly still regarded as a Royalist at heart, since he was briefly imprisoned in 1659 in the aftermath of Booth's Rising in favour of the exiled King.

Restoration

At the Restoration of Charles II Marley, despite his questionable loyalties, had little to fear from the new regime: The King's promise of mercy to his opponents in the Declaration of Breda was generously fulfilled in the

Indemnity and Oblivion Act 1660. Acts of mercy however could not redeem Marley's ruined reputation. He was elected to the Commons in 1661 as MP for Newcastle, but quickly found that his betrayal had not been forgiven or forgotten. A petition was sent to the Commons, directly accusing him of treason, and he was suspended from the House. Charles II, true to his policy of reconciliation, sent a message asking the House to forgive Marlay for his "infirmities", and to recover their former "good opinion" of him. Marlay also became Mayor of Newcastle again for the last time in 1661.

He was allowed to resume his seat in the Commons, but after this disastrous start to his national career he never made his mark as a politician, and for the rest of his life had to endure accusations of being a traitor. Although he was appointed to a number of committees, he made only one recorded speech in the House in his 12 years as a member (although even this puts him slightly above the average: Kenyon notes that the great majority of MPs in the seventeenth century never once opened their mouths at Westminster). Even his conduct during the Siege of Newcastle was questioned, and there were wild accusations that he had been bribed to betray the town.

By 1665 he was prospering again. Hearth Tax records for that year show his house had more than ten hearths. The average for another merchant Hostmen was 5.7.

Reputation

While his courage and determination at Newcastle won him some respect, contemporaries in general had little good to say of him. Sir George Downing said that Marley "belonged to anyone who spoke kindly to him". The Earl of Northumberland dismissed him as a "cuckold and a knave". In 1671 Sam Hartlib, a son of the renowned scholar Samuel Hartlib, who apparently blamed Marley for persecuting his father (who had died in poverty), insulted him at the door of the House of Commons, calling him "less than the dust beneath my feet". He was noted for his hostility to Puritanism.

Sir John died in Newcastle in 1673 and was buried on 24 October in St George's Porch of St Nicholas's Church, now Newcastle Cathedral.

Family and memorials

He married Mary Mitford, of whose marital fidelity Lord Northumberland spoke so unkindly, and they had several sons. Of his children, most is known of Anthony, who moved to Ireland and became a prosperous landowner. Many of his Irish descendants achieved distinction, notably Thomas Marlay, Lord Chief Justice of Ireland, and the statesman Henry Grattan. The family name is commemorated in Marlay Park, a popular amenity near Dublin city; the prominent banker David La Touche, who built Marlay House, named it for his wife Elizabeth Marlay, Sir John's great-granddaughter.

Roger Thornton

His early years are clouded in mystery but historians of note state that he was the son of Hodgkin Thornton and was born in Witton, Northumberland. Others attribute his origins as being in the Hartburn area, that could be influenced by the existence of hamlets of East and West Thornton (now farms) existing at that time

The Reverend Edward Rust, the Rector of Redmarshall in his 1929 book "Roger Thornton" gives his father's name as Rob. In his preface to the book the worthy Reverend asserts that his work is based on known facts, unfortunately he fails to provide the source details and Newcastle Central Library who hold a reference copy have apparently filed it as a novel.

This is a shame for Reverend Rust tells an entertaining tale and even if some of the contents may be poetic licence it cannot be denied that the man himself was an entertaining character.

Whatever the truth it remains a fact that towards the end of the 1300's young Roger made his way to Newcastle, he was probably quite a young man at the time, possibly a teenager. As one of the 4 bailiffs in 1382 was a John Thornton and as Roger himself in time became a bailiff it may be reasonable to suspect that there was some family connection and this may be the cause for this young country boy to uproots and make for the bright lights of the big town.

Having cast a little doubt on the proven accuracy of his report I would nevertheless love to believe the Reverend Rust's account of Roger's arrival at the outskirts of the town. What he says (in summary) is:

With only a halfpenny to his name, the coat he was wearing (a hap) and with an Iambs skin to trade it seems that Roger arrived at the Westgate of the town walls (Roughly the Bath Lane junction with Westgate Road). We are told by the Reverend Rust that the gatekeeper was one Cuddy Wakeman and apparently, he was a real "Jobsworth". Roger is said to have reached the boundary of the town just as the gates were about to close for the night and no amount of pleading would prevent Cuddy Wakeman from doing his job and refusing entry.

The gate was duly slammed in Roger's face, luckily for him however a passing pitman "Geordie Robson" took pity on him and took him to his already overcrowded home on the outskirts of Newcastle and gave him food and lodging.

Refreshed Roger returned to the gate the next day and entered Newcastle and never looked back.

A delightful story, if only we could prove its truth.

What is certain however is that by 1394 Roger Thornton was on public record as a "shipman" and was part owner of "The Good Year". This ship and its cargo were seized by the people of Wismar and Rostock in what we now know as Northern Germany. In due course compensation was paid so Roger was not out of pocket for too long.

In 1397 Roger himself was a bailiff in Newcastle, he married a wealthy heiress Agnes Wanton. By 1399 he was representing Newcastle in Parliament, it must be remembered that in those days Parliament only met when summoned by the monarch and then usually to raise a tax or an army. The King in question at the time was Henry Bolingbroke who on defeating Richard II had become Henry IV. Roger also represented Newcastle in Parliament in 1411, 1417 and 1419.

Roger is on record as being a keen supporter of Henry IV and played a part in the King's defeat of Harry Hotspur, the same Harry Hotspur who now stands above him in Northumberland Street.

He went on to be part of the team which persuaded the King to make Newcastle a town independent of the County of Northumberland at which point his title of bailiff became that of Sheriff. He became the first mayor under the new arrangement and indeed became mayor on no less than nine occasions.

All of this political campaigning however did not deter him from his shipping pursuits. In 1400 he was a merchant of wool to Flanders and other ports. There have been suggestions that his ships were involved in some piracy at the time but I cannot state whether or not that was true.

From 1406 the King authorised Roger to receive customs revenue for the port of Newcastle, by 1422 he was shipping coal out of Newcastle.

All of this activity certainly made him a wealthy and powerful man but he believed in giving as much as he took or very close to it. In 1403 he was given the kings licence to found the House of God to provide food and clothing to the poor and needy. In 1412, on the death of his wife, he built Maison Dieu which was the Hospital of St Katherine otherwise known as Thornton's Hospital, it was designed to accommodate 9 men and 4 women.

The antiquary Leland described him as 'the richest merchant that ever was dwelling in Newcastle'

Certainly, the records show that in 1385 he exported wool, in 1389 lambskins and cloth by 1393

By 1400 he received a royal licence with others to buy 2,000 sacks of wool for shipment to Flanders, there was a condition that the consignment had to come from wool grown beyond the Tees, which was generally of a rather inferior quality, and, in the event, was left to rot on the quays of Newcastle because of new government restrictions.

Two further licences for the export of 600 sarplars (A large bale or package of wool, containing eighty tods or 2,240 pounds in weight.) and 2,000 sacks were, however, issued to Thornton and his partners in 1408 and 1410, so they were able to salvage some of their losses.

Even so, the Newcastle woolmen continued to face serious competition from the merchants of the Calais, who were determined to retain their monopoly over English wool exports at all costs; and Thornton must have chafed at the limitations imposed upon him.

His desire to operate in a more open market no doubt encouraged him to invest in the rapidly expanding coal and lead trade of the north-east. He regularly exported cargoes of coal in ships from both Newcastle and Schiedam; and in 1422 he was commissioned by the government to purchase 100 keels of sea coal in the north for sale in London.

At some unknown date he actually acquired a messuage in 'Secolelane' in the City of London, presumably as a base for his dealings with the merchants there.

Even more money was to be made out of lead, which soon became Thornton's chief commercial preoccupation. He was already exporting it as early as 1389, but his involvement really developed in 1401, when he negotiated a 12-year lease of the Bishop of Durham's lead mines in Weardale. (These mines also produced silver, which Thornton shipped overseas for a handsome profit.)

In 1406, in consideration of his work for the Crown, he received a grant of lead, which he used as currency for other transactions.

Even the marriage of his daughter, Isabel, to John, the son and heir of his parliamentary colleague, Sir John Middleton, was partly financed in this way.

The contract specified that he would pay £200 in gold together with nearly eight tons of lead, receiving in return a lease of whatever estates were to be settled upon the young couple by the Middletons.

Not surprisingly, his will consists largely of bequests of sizeable quantities of lead to neighbouring religious houses and churches. Yet in common with most medieval merchants, Thornton still sought to diversify his investments by trading in a wide range of commodities such as woad, madder and wine.

In 1407, for example, he imported 49 tuns of wine into Newcastle, some of which undoubtedly found its way into the cellars of Durham priory. The accounts of the priory record purchases from him of red Gascon wine in 1404 and 1423, as well as noting payments for Spanish iron and lead from his warehouses. Yet not all of his ventures proved so successful.

One serious reversal occurred in 1394, when, as briefly touched on earlier he joined with a consortium of Newcastle merchants in loading the *Goodyear* with a valuable cargo of wool and wine. The ship was attacked by pirates from Wismer and Rostock, who not only seized the merchandise but also imprisoned some of Thornton's associates. Despite their strenuous protests, it was not until 1405 that Henry IV sent an embassy to obtain satisfaction.

Being a man of many talents, Thornton proved himself invaluable as a conscientious royal servant and municipal official. Mayor of Newcastle nine times, he was regularly named among the 12 *probi homines* who chose the parliamentary representatives for the borough, being present at ten elections, if not more, between 1414 and 1427. He was also one of the delegates who travelled to Durham, in March 1412, in an unsuccessful attempt to settle a protracted dispute with Bishop Langley over the building of a tower by the townspeople on the south side of the Tyne bridge.

In recognition of his work for the Crown as a customs officer and commissioner, Thornton received many generous rewards. In 1405, while mayor of Newcastle, he had kept the town secure against the rebel forces of the Earl of Northumberland, reputedly at a cost of some 1,000 marks to himself.

To make good these losses, he secured from Henry IV the manors of Acklam and Kirklevington in Yorkshire along with other, smaller properties confiscated from the earl.

Although he later restored Acklam to a former tenant, Thornton retained Kirklevington until his death, 25 years later. His commitment to the Lancastrian regime was again acknowledged during the aftermath of Henry, Lord Scrope of Masham's execution for treason in 1415. On this occasion he shared with William Massy the keepership of Scrope's Northumberland estates, at an annual farm of £24.

Other grants from the Crown included the goods and merchandise of certain Livonian traders, which he was allowed to keep in repayment of two loans of £100 each made in about 1410 to the prince of Wales and the government.

That Thornton had already begun to accumulate sizeable estates of his own is evident from the award to him at the same time (in return for a fine of 250 marks) of a general pardon for 'all acquisitions and alienations of lands held in chief and entries therein without licence and all debts, accounts and arrears'. Furthermore, in 1424, he secured from the Exchequer the lease of the manor of Riplington in Northumberland for the next ten years.

Leland observed that Thornton was 'first a merchant and then a landed man'; and his investments were clearly made out of the profits of trade. Between 1406 and 1411, for example, he built up substantial holdings in and around the manor of Netherwitton in Northumberland, while at the same date acquiring the manor of Byker from Sir Richard Arundel.

Later in life, Thornton set aside some of his land in Byker to support such philanthropic ventures such as the foundation of St. Katherine's hospital in Newcastle, and a chantry at the church of All Saints there.

Another opportunity for expansion came in November 1421, on the marriage of his daughter, Isabel, to the young John Middleton, whose family permitted him to farm their manors of Jesmond and East Swinburn, together with land in Cramlington, Crooked Oak and Newbiggin, for the next ten years.

Thornton's estates in Northumberland also included the manors of Great Benton, Stannington, Plessey and Shotton, as well as farmland in Belasis and Trenwell. His interests as a landowner extended into the palatinate of Durham, where, from 1409 onwards he set about consolidating his position. He began by purchasing property in Coldcoats, Ingoe, Whickham and Gateshead; and by 1411 he had taken possession of the manor of Redhugh and certain franchises in Axwell.

His title to the latter was questioned in 1420, although he managed to retain hold of the manor of Axwell pending a decision in the court of his former adversary, Bishop Langley of Durham. Other piecemeal acquisitions included the manors of Swalwell and Ludworth and holdings in Herrington and Darlington.

Thornton was, of course, much in demand as a trustee, and over the years he was a party to many conveyances of land by his fellow burgesses and local landowners, such as Sir William Swinburne's widow, Mary. His other associates in these ventures included John Wall, William Ellerby and Robert Whelpington all of whom were involved with him in financial transactions.

Needless to say, Thornton ranked among the leading property owners in the town of Newcastle, where he bought many gardens, tenements and leases. His own mansion in the 'Broadchare' must have appeared sumptuous to his neighbours, especially as it was furnished with luxury goods from London.

Indeed, with the passage of time and the spectacular growth of his commercial profits, Thornton actually began to invest in the London property market, purchasing four cottages and a house in 'Thurnagrayelane' and part of a messuage in Cheapside, as well as the above-mentioned base in 'Secolelane' where he transacted business.

Evidence of his standing in the northern community is to be found in the marriage contracts which he negotiated for his two children: as we have already seen, the first of these brought his daughter a husband from one of the leading gentry families in Northumberland, while the second provided the Thorntons with a lasting and important baronial connexion.

In February 1429, Thornton's sole surviving son and heir, Roger, was betrothed to Elizabeth, daughter of John, Lord Greystoke; and although the merchant was obliged to settle an extremely large estate upon the young couple, the social *cachet* which he thus acquired must have seemed worth every penny.

But not all of Thornton's great wealth was employed in furthering his earthly career. From quite early on in life he had evidently felt a strong sense of civic responsibility which, coupled with a desire to ensure the speedy passage of his soul through purgatory, led him to spend generously on pious works.

His most notable endowment was St. Katherine's hospital in Newcastle, a work begun in 1402 with the award of a royal licence, and completed some ten years later. The hospital, which was clearly influenced by some of the impressive projects then being undertaken in London, was intended as a home for nine poor men and four poor women under the supervision of a chaplain.

Despite the scale of his original grant of land and money, funds must have proved inadequate, for in 1424 Thornton obtained permission from the government to settle additional rents worth £7 p.a. upon his foundation, which he had by then placed in the care of the civic authorities.

Roger Thornton made his will on 22 Dec. 1429 at his house in the 'Broadchare', and died on 3 Jan. following. He was buried beside his late wife at All Saints' church, Newcastle, under a fine brass, executed in the Flemish tradition. He had already founded a chantry in the church, to which he now made a number of handsome bequests.

Many religious foundations benefited from Thornton's generosity; and houses throughout the north-east were enriched by gifts of money or lead. The magnificent east window portraying the 12 apostles at St. Nicholas's church, Newcastle, which one local antiquary regarded as an example of 'the later form of English architecture in its most just and beautiful proportions', was but one of his endowments.

In gratitude for the lead which provided him with a new roof for the abbey church, the abbot of Newminster arranged for daily masses to be said for the soul of his late benefactor. To his hospital 'ye *maison dieu* of Saint Kateryne of my foundation' Thornton left £20 in cash, although enough goods and specie remained to make his son and heir, Roger, a very wealthy man indeed.

The Mad Martins of Haydon Bridge

Background

The work of an ancient tanner was unglamorous to say the least. It started with an arduous preparatory stage that could take several weeks.

First, the animal's skins were cleaned and softened with water. Once cleaned, the tanners still had to pound the hides to remove excess fat and flesh. Next, to loosen the hair follicles, they would either coat the hides with an alkaline lime mixture, leave the hides out to putrefy for months, or soak them in vats of urine before removal with a dull knife (scudding).

In the bating stage, tanners worked animal dung or brains into the skins either by beating with sticks or kneading them in a vat of faeces and water. The combination of bacteria enzymes found in animal waste and the beating or kneading action fermented the skin and made it supple.

Understandably, ancient tanneries were always found on the outskirts of towns.

With the malodorous preparatory work complete, the hides were ready for tanning. From ancient times and through the 18th century, tanners used a chemical compound called tannin, derived from tree bark and certain plant leaves. Hides were stretched out on frames and immersed in vats concentrated amounts of tannin. Tannins bind to the collagen proteins in the hide and coat them, causing them to become less water-soluble, more bacteria-resistant, and more flexible.

The most famous tanner in the premises at Tow House, close to Bardon Mill was William Fenwick Martin, more commonly known as Fenwick Martin.

He was, to say the least a character. His own father William born in 1699 had been born in Whitfield Hall, at that time it was still owned by the Whitfield family an old Norman family who had been granted its residence in the 12th century. By 1750 however it was sold to the Ord family or more particularly William Ord of Fenham the High Sheriff of Newcastle upon Tyne.

Old William Martin and his wife Mary Lowes married in 1734 and their children included Matthew 1737, Hugh 1743 William Fenwick Martin 1744 and Mary 1746.

It is of course William Fenwick Martin who is of interest to us, usually known as Fenwick he was described as a wild spirited fellow from Tow House.

Fenwick had fallen head over heels in love with Isabella Thompson, she appears to have been brought up as a genteel young lady born in 1751.

Her father was Richard Thompson who owned a small holding at Lands' End in Haydon Bridge. Her mother was Ann Ridley who believed that her family was descended from the protestant martyr Nicholas Ridley.

It is certainly true that Nicholas Ridley was a local boy made good, he had been born in Tynedale and educated at the Royal Grammar School, Newcastle.

***Nicholas Ridley** (c. 1500–16 October 1555) was an English Bishop of London (the only bishop called "Bishop of London and Westminster"[1]). Ridley was burned at the stake as one of the Oxford Martyrs during the Marian Persecutions for his teachings and his support of Lady Jane Grey. He is remembered with a commemoration in the calendar of saints in some parts of the Anglican Communion on 16 October.*

Richard and Ann Thompson were far from keen on Isabella's new boyfriend. Indeed, their opposition was so strong that in 1771 the couple eloped to Gretna Green and married by a blacksmith over the anvil.

They did return to Northumberland and apparently made up with the Thompsons and went through a church service at Holy Cross, Haltwhistle.

The illustration is of the church prior to its restoration in 1870

Fenwick seems to have had many career changes and as he appears to have been a great promoter of himself some descriptions I originally took with a pinch of salt.

He was variously: a tanner (Yes, he was)

He quelled a mutiny during the American War of Independence (He certainly served in the army in that war which lasted from 1775 to 1783 and it is in fact on record that he was injured in quelling a mutiny within the ranks and was retired from active duty after only three months. As a result of that he was on the register of Chelsea Pensioners)

He kept an Inn at Hartley between Whitley Bay and Blyth. It is thought that this may in fact be the Astley Arms

He worked as a woodman to a Mr Tulip at Highside near Lowgate. Two miles from Hexham

He gave fencing lessons at The Old Globe yard at Battle Hill in Hexham and billed himself as "the best swordsman in the country"

He travelled the countryside as a pedlar and drove cattle to London. A little more information about that. Isabella was a wealthy woman in her own right and he took a large portion of that money to buy goods to sell as and where he could. This was while she was in Scotland visiting her parents, more of the reason they were in Scotland in Chapter one. As regards driving cattle to London, yes, he did as he had never seen London and this was an opportunity to do so

In between all that he played a part in aiding Isabella to have thirteen children only five of which lived to adulthood.

The truly important thing about Fenwick is that after his wedding he set up (or was set up by his father-in-law) as a tanner in Tow House.

At that time Tow House was just that a large house with extensive grounds with a few other properties, around the property. It had been in the ownership of the Thompson family

The building will have been allowed to fall to rack and ruin after he left it and the land was not built on until 1870 by which time the smell will have faded making living there acceptable. The nature of tanning is that several holes in the surrounding land will have been dug for the leather to lay in and mature so the land will have been extensive.

The sons of Fenwick and Isabella were described by Thomas Carlyle "The Martins are all wildish in the head" I will leave it to you to decide if this is an accurate description

It was in the cottage attached to the Tannery in Tow House that William Martin was born.

William Martin

William Martin was born at Tow House, one of a group of old Greystone cottages standing on a plateau half a mile west of Bardon Mill during a night of violent thunder and lightning on June 21st 1772. Given his date of birth we can surmise the urgency in his parent's mind to marry and the sudden willingness of his grandparents to bless and formalise the wedding.

We know that in 1775 Fenwick was representing his country in America and the care of William fell very much onto his maternal grandparents the Thompsons who also in 1775 moved to a farm in Kintyre in Western Scotland. The reason was that the Duke of Argyll had issued a request for experienced English farmers to come and teach animal husbandry to his tenant farmers

On the death of his grandparents, William went to live with his father, then in business at Ayr. There he says he often saw 'the celebrated Scotch bard, Robert Burns,' and he adds, 'I think I never saw him sober—to my knowledge.'

In 1794 he was working in a ropery at Howdon dock, Wallsend, and in the following year he joined the Northumberland regiment of militia at Durham.

On his discharge in 1805 he attained a patent for shoes, and began to study the concept of perpetual motion, and discovered it after thirty-seven different inventions,' including original contrivances for fan ventilators, safety lamps, and railways.

The pretensions of Sir Humphry Davy and George Stephenson to discoveries in the same field he denounced as dishonest, and he also claimed to have confuted Newton's theory of gravitation.

Martin proceeded in 1808 to London, where he exhibited and sold (for an absurdly small sum) his foolish and redundant patent for perpetual motion (see DIRK'S, *Perpetuum Mobile*, 2nd ser. p. 200). He sold it for £5, it could be seen working for the next twenty-eight years before disappearing.

In the following year he returned to his modest trade of rope-making, and in 1810 to the militia. Passing over to Ireland with his regiment, he made shift to acquire during his moments of leisure the elements of line engraving.

Despite his quackery and buffoonery, Martin possessed much ingenuity as a mechanician (*the word used in the research I found*), and in 1814 was presented with the Isis silver medal by the Society of Arts for the invention of a spring weighing machine with circular dial and index.

In the same year he married 'a celebrated dressmaker,' whom he also describes as 'an inoffensive woman' (she died 16 Jan. 1832), and founded the 'Martinean Society,' based, in opposition to the Royal Society, upon the negation of the Newtonian theory of gravitation.

In 1821 he published 'A New System of Natural Philosophy on the Principle of Perpetual Motion, with a Variety of other Useful Discoveries.' He henceforth styled himself 'Anti-Newtonian,' and commenced a series of lectures setting forth his views in the Newcastle district.

In 1830 he made an extended lecturing tour throughout England, from which he returned triumphant, declaring that no one had dared to defend the Newtonian system.

In 1833 he issued in his followers' behoof 'A Short Outline of the Philosopher's Life, from being a Child in Frocks to the Present Day, after the Defeat of all Impostors, False Philosophers, since the Creation. ... The Burning of York Minster is not left out, and an Account of the Four Brothers and one Sister.'

The British Museum copy contains a number of manuscript additions by the author. In 1837 he exhibited in Newcastle an ingenious mail carriage to be propelled upon rails by means of a winch and toothed wheel.

He was at this time residing at Wallsend, from whence he issued periodically his lucubration's with the signature 'Wm. Martin, Nat. Phil. and Poet.'

He affected extreme singularity of attire, and hawked his books or exhibited his inventions among the Northumbrian miners.

His later mechanical efforts—some undoubtedly both useful and ingenious—included models for a lifeboat and a lifebuoy, a self-acting railway gate, and a design for a high-level bridge over the Tyne.

His last days were passed in comfort at his brother John's house at Chelsea, where he died on 9 Feb. 1851.

Martin's chief printed works—all published at Newcastle—are, exclusive of single sheets and minor pamphlets:

1. 'Harlequin's Invasion, a new Pantomine [*sic*] engraved and published by W. M.,' 1811, 8vo.

2. 'A New Philosophical Song or Poem Book, called the Northumberland Bard, or the Downfall of all False Philosophy,' 1827, 8vo.

3. 'W. M.'s Challenge to the whole Terrestrial Globe as a Philosopher and Critic, and Poet and Prophet, showing the Travels of his Mind, the quick Motion of the Soul,' &c. (verse) [1829], 8vo; 2nd edit. 1829.

4. 'The Christian Philosopher's Explanation of the General Deluge, and the Proper Cause of all the Different Strata,' 1834, 8vo.

5. 'The Thunder Storm of Dreadful Forked Lightning; God's Judgement against all False Teachers. ... Including an Account of the Railway Phenomenon, the Wonder of the World!' 1837.

6. 'The Defeat of the Eighth Scientific Meeting of the British Association of Asses, which we may properly call the Rich Folks' Hopping, or the False Philosophers in an Uproar' [1838], 8vo.

7. 'Light and Truth, M.'s Invention for Destroying all Foul Air and Fire Damps in Coal Pits, [proving also] the Scriptures to be right which learned Men are mystifying, and proving the Orang-outang or Monkey, the most unlikely thing under the Sun to be the Serpent that Beguiled our First Parents,' 1838, 8vo.

8. 'An Exposure of a New System of Irreligion ... called the New Moral World, promulgated by R. Owen, Esq., whose Doctrine proves him a Child of the Devil,' 1839, 8vo.

9. 'W. Martin, Christian Philosopher. The Exposure of Dr. Nichol, the Impostor and Mock Astronomer of Glasgow College' [1839], 8vo.

10. 'W. Martin, Philosophical Conqueror of all Nations. Also, a Challenge for all College Professors to prove this Wrong, and themselves Right, and that Air is not the first great Cause of all Things Animate and Inanimate,' verse [1846], 8vo.

Jonathan Martin

Thomas Carlyle's description of the Martin brothers in that they are all "wildish in the head was probably most true of Jonathan.

He was born in 1782 at Highside House near Hexham. The ultra-religious grandparents and mother brought all of the children up in a strict Methodist type tradition with a strong sense of hellfire and damnation.

He was unable to speak until he was six due to a malformation of his tongue.

His life seemed to have been full of drama. On one occasion he fell into a trough and his sister Ann had to seize his feet and pull him out, another time playing near some lead mines he blindfolded himself and was walking around until his sister called "Oh brother stop there is a pit before you" Removing his blindfold he found himself right on the ledge of a huge shaft.

A more serious incident however occurred when he was with another sister. Two boys were arguing with the two daughters of a neighbour Peggy Hobuck. Mrs Hobuck came out of her house to investigate the noise. The boys ran away but Mrs Hobuck seized Jonathan's sister and flung her down some stairs.

Another neighbour came out and said "Oh Peggy Hobuck how could you be so cruel?" Mrs Hobuck did not answer and went back into her house.

Jonathans sister said "Oh Dolly don't tell my mother that Peggy threw me down some stairs for she will think I did something amiss"

The sister died some days later after much suffering.

At the funeral Peggy Hobuck passed herself off very well but then her conscience began playing on her and she confessed. She was sentenced to prison and died a miserable death,

Jonathans reaction was to pray for his sister's soul as he feared she must have sinned. Such was the effect of the fire and brimstone teaching.

After that he hated where he lived and persuaded his parents to let him move to the farm of an uncle where he helped look after the sheep,

After that he worked as an apprentice tanner until 1804 when he moved to London with a vague idea of visiting other countries, his dream became true as he was press ganged into the navy. He left in around 1811

In 1812 he married Martha Carter and they had a son who they called Richard after one of his brothers. His parents both died in 1813. Before her death Isabella had a dream in which she found that her son's names would resound around the world.

Isabella then appeared after death in a dream to Jonathan where she warned him that he would be hanged. That experience reinvigorated his religious fervour. He became a Wesleyan Methodist and had contempt for the priests of the Church of England who in his mind constantly attended balls and concerts.

In 1818 there are records of him interrupting church services and being pulled from the church by a constable and being arrested for vagrancy.

Matters escalated from there and he planned to shoot the Bishop of Oxford,

His wife discovered his plan and hid the gun. Being unable to find the gun next day he took that as a sign that he should not go ahead with the shooting.

His plot however was discovered and he was sentenced to be "confined to the mad house for life." He was taken to the lunatic asylum at West Auckland. He was treated badly at West Auckland by a drunken guard and was moved to Gateshead asylum and shortly after his arrival was allowed to walk the garden.

He decided to extend his stroll beyond the bounds of the asylum as a means of convincing the authorities that he could look after himself.

On his inevitable recapture he was placed in chains and spent many days filing away at the chains. Having released himself he walked 20 miles or so to Acomb where a relative Edward Kell had a farm Edward helped remove the remaining manacle and gave him shelter. When the constable came looking for him, he managed to evade capture and travelled variously to Edinburgh, Wallsend, Bishop Auckland and planned to go to London,

En-Route he found work at Boroughbridge Darlington and Hull, While at Boroughbridge he heard that his wife had died and his house ransacked.

He evaded capture for eight years.

In May 1828 in Boston, Lincolnshire he met Maria Hudson, at 27 she was 20 years younger than him. They married October 19th that year in Boston Church. He refused to pay the clergyman's fee,

By now he had written his autobiography entitled "Life" and subsisted by selling copies for between 2d and 6d. He was also in the habit of pinning notices on church doors reading: *"Oh, hear the word of the Lord ye clergymen and tremble for the fay of vengeance is at hand. Howl and weep for your time is at an end. You have long deceived the people but now be ashamed of yourselves"*

On December 26th he left his son Richard at boarding school in Lincoln and he and his new wife Maria travelled to York where they took lodgings at 60 Adwick, the home of William Lawn a shoe maker. On December 27th he wrote the first of 5 letters to York clergy, the content is similar in all, this was the first: (including his spelling)

"I right O Clergymen to you to warn you to fly from the Roth to cum, you who are bringing a grievance upon the land you blind giels and deceivers of the people. How can you esape the damnation of Hell you whitent spa pulkirs you who are dragging millions of souls to hell with you.

Will not the rych and the myty have to curs the day that they sat under your blind and halish doctrine.

But I warn you to repent and cry for mercy for the sorde of justis is at hand and your gret churchis and ministaris will come rattling down upon your gilty heads for the son of Boney Part is preparing for you and he will finish the work his father left undun   Jonthn Martin   Your sinsear friend No 60 Aldwick

I should explain that he had many dreams of the future and in one the son of Napoleon Bonaparte with a great army invaded England declaring war on the clergy.

His letters went unanswered despite signing them and giving his address.

He had yet another dream in which he conversed with God as to what action he should take next and he believed that God advised him to burn York Minster.

On January 27th 1829 Jonathan and Maria travelled to Leeds and took lodgings but on January 31st Jonathan alone returned to 60 Aldwick, York.

On Sunday February 1st he worshipped at a Methodist Chapel and then went to a cook shop where he bought two pence worth of bread and soup.

At 3.30 that afternoon when the sexton Job Knowles arrived to open the York Minster, he found Jonathan waiting at the south entrance. The service began at 4pm.

Jonathan said later that he was annoyed that the prayers and singing of the amens did not come from the heart.

He was also annoyed that the clergy and the congregation needed to refer to their prayer books, he also complained that the organ had a buzzing noise.

The service ended at 5pm. Jonathan hid in the north Transept and lay down beside the statue of Archbishop Greenfield.

Job Knowles locked up at 6.30pm Following, what he said, was instructions from God, Jonathan took a candle and lit it using a small piece of flint and a tinder box he had purloined from his lodgings. He then cut 90 feet of rope from the belfry to create a form of ladder, He used that to access the choir area.

According to him God then told him to take a bible so that he would have something to read while in prison. Next, he cut down the curtains from around the Archbishop's throne, the fringe of the pulpit hangers and the curtain at the north end of the stalls.

Then he set fire to the material he had gathered, He made his escape by cutting away the lead from a window using pinchers again stolen from William Lawn.

The fire was not discovered until 7am next morning, Once the alarm was raised 12 fire engines were despatched from as far away as Leeds.

The Leeds engine was delayed when a wheel fell off.

Another was slowed when one of the horses pulling it dropped dead.

A third overturned as it turned the corner into Minster Yard.

Ironically a lady viewing the blaze observed that it could have been a scene painted by the noted artist John Martin.

60 Aldwick was searched but Jonathan was not there.

Maria was captured in Leeds selling copies of his biography "Life."

A £100 fine was issued for his apprehension, one of those who began searching was William Stainthorpe both an inn keeper and a sheriff's officer.

Presumably, basing his hunch on information gathered from "Life" he made his way north, initially searching the property of a member of the Thompson family at Wall Barnes, he then made his way to Codlaw Hill the home of Jonathans friend and relative Edward Kell.

Jonathan was sitting waiting and gave no resistance.

The Tyne Mercury on Tuesday 10th February announced that he had been captured the previous Friday.

In March 1829 he stood trial at York Castle before Baron Hullock and a jury. The case drew nationwide attention coming only two months after the Burke and Hare trial.

Jonathan was defended by Lord Henry Brougham who had defended the notorious Queen Caroline in 1821 in her divorce from King George IV.

His services were paid for by brothers John and Richard. The jury found him guilty, the penalty was a death sentence as it was a capital offence however the judge ruled him not guilty on the grounds of insanity,

He was detained in Bethlam Royal Hospital nicknamed Bedlam. He remained there until his death 9 years later. Following his death his son Richard wrote to his uncle William advising him of this death

30, Allsop Terrace, New Road, London, May 31st 1838

MY DEAR UNCLE,

I do not write to you often, and when I do so I have only to communicate occurrences of a melancholy nature. Last year wrote and told you of your brother Richard's decease, and how I have to announce that my poor father was released from his bodily confinement; his spirit has escaped the boundaries of his prison walls, and returned to Him who gave it, and whom this earth he made it his duty to diligently serve.

When we take into consideration the unfortunate circumstances under which he was placed, and think upon the pleasures dear to him from which was effectually debarred,— only in his thoughts visiting the scenes of his childhood, and his friends in the north, of whom he often spoke, and often wished to visit,—retaining the love he had of roaming the flowery fields, and visiting the pleasant haunts of his youth,—

it is but natural to suppose that he inwardly fretted, though never complained.

Being as he was prepared to meet his God, he anticipated with pleasure his coming release, which took place on Sunday, May 27th, after three days' illness. Knowing the happy state of mind in which he died, we are in some degree reconciled to his loss, though I shall feel his loss very much, and at being deprived of the melancholy pleasure of visiting him in his prison.

My aunt Atkinson (this is Ann the only sister of the Martins who reached adulthood) and I were there on the Monday, two days before he was taken ill: he was delighted to see us, and appeared cheerful and contented; he talked about his friends in the north, and asked if we had heard from you, and hoped that you were doing well.

He had got permission to draw a little, which he had not been allowed to do for a long time [other reports suggest that when he drew the subject was always York Minster and it left him in a manic state, which is why he was not given the materials]. I left him paper, &c. and he began with eagerness, and must have worked very hard it; for he would not get the paper until Tuesday morning, and Wednesday it was that he felt himself ill and gave his drawing and everything up to his keeper, and said he was assured that he would not require them anymore, and he would only read his Bible. In that short time, he had half covered a large sheet of drawing paper with a serpent, lions, archers shooting, and other things which I do not remember, as I have not the drawing yet.

He did not keep to his bed until Saturday when he felt himself a great deal worse, especially towards the night. The keeper came and told us the condition he was in. My uncle and I immediately went to see him, but he was in state of lethargy and insensible to everything around. He did not know us.

We remained with him until twelve o'clock, but he continued in the same state, and remained so until about an hour before his death, when he revived and retained the use

his faculties and reason: and, when being told that he would rally and get better, smiled and said "Oh no, I feel much worse, I shall soon be released now," and then laid his head Back the pillow and expired like one going into quiet slumber—truly his end was peace.

You, my dear uncle, will be much grieved at losing a brother to whom you were so strongly attached, and who retained for you the strongest affection; but I trust we shall meet where affectionate brothers, relatives, and friends will never part.

With the kindest loves all the family, aunt Atkinson, Mr. Warren, uncle, aunt, &c. I conclude, and remain my dear uncle, your affectionate nephew,

RICHARD MARTIN.

Sadly, just three months later this Richard himself the only son of Jonathan committed suicide

One other point is worth mentioning, during the excavations of York Minster in order to restore it, it was observed that a Norman crypt was in fact larger than had been surmised, work was carried out and that resulted in the Undercroft a popular visiting area today for those visiting York Minster

The contemporary account from The Newgate Calendar

JONATHAN MARTIN

A Madman who Set Fire to York Minster.

The name of this wretched maniac will long be remembered from the circumstance of the object of his offence being that of burning down that venerable monument of antiquity -- York Minster; an effort in which, happily, he only partially succeeded.

The fire was discovered in a most remarkable manner. On the evening of Sunday the 1st of February, 1829, one of the choristers, a lad named Swainbank, was passing through the Minster-yard, when, setting his foot on a piece of ice, he was thrown on his back, on the ground.

Before he had time to rise, he perceived smoke proceeding from the building before him. He at once gave the alarm, and assistance was immediately procured; but it was not until the choir, with its magnificent organ and its beautiful roof, had been totally destroyed, that the flames could be conquered.

At first this national catastrophe was supposed to have been the result of accident; but the discovery of one of the bell-pulls, knotted so as to form a species of ladder, suspended from one of the windows of the building, and of evidence of a light having been seen moving about in the belfry after all the officers of the Minster had retired, on the night of the fire, led to a conclusion that it was the work of an incendiary.

This belief was on the following week strengthened by the apprehension of a person named Jonathan Martin, at Leeds, with some portion of the velvet from the reading-desk in his possession.

He was examined before the magistrates, and at once confessed that he had set fire to the building in obedience to the will of the Lord communicated to him in two remarkable dreams. He was committed to York Castle for trial, and it turned out that he had been already twice in confinement as a madman, and that he had prophesied the destruction of the Minster.

On Monday, the 30th of March, he took his trial at the York assizes, and was found by the jury to have been of unsound mind at the time of his committing the offence charged against him.

The following extracts from his defence at once showed that he was a religious enthusiast: --

When called upon for his defence, he proceeded to say, in a Northern dialect and with great energy –

"Well, sir, the first impression that I had about it was from a dream. And after I had written five letters to these clergy, the last of which I believe was a very severe one, and all of which I dated from my lodgings at No.90, Aldwick, I was very anxious to speak to them by word of mouth; but none of them would come near me.

So, I prayed to the Lord, and asked him what was to be done. And I dreamed that I saw a cloud come over the cathedral -- and it tolled towards me at my lodgings; it awoke me out of my sleep, and I asked the Lord what it meant; and he told me it was to warn these clergymen of England, who were going to plays, and cards, and such like: and the Lord told me he had chosen me to warn them, and reminded me of the prophecies -- that there should in the latter days be signs in the heavens.

I felt so impressed with it, that I found the Lord had destined me to show those people the way to flee from the wrath to come.

Then I bethought me that I could not do that job without being out all night, and I considered whether I should let my wife know.

I got everything ready, and I took the ring from my wife's finger, and talked to her about what I have mentioned -- and I told her what I meant to do: she grieved very much, and I had work to get off.

I still staid a few days, but I could get no rest whatever until I had accomplished the work.

It was a severe contest between flesh and blood -- and then I bethought me what would come of her and my son Richard, who I had at Lincoln, Then the Lord said unto me, 'What thou does, do with all thy might.'

I tore from her and said, 'Well, well, Lord -- Not my will but Thine be done.'

I then left Leeds, taking twenty of my books with me; but I had no money, and went into Tadcaster; there I got a gill of ale.

[He then proceeded to state the manner in which he travelled and supported himself to York.]

On Sunday (February 1st) I went to the cathedral service, and it vexed me to hear them singing their prayers and amens.

I knew it did not come from the heart, it was deceiving the people. Then there was the organ, buz! huz! and said I to mysen, I'll hae thee down to-night, thou shot buz no more!

well, they were all going out, and I lay me down by't side of the Bishop's round by the pillar.

[The prisoner concealed himself behind a tomb, between which and the wall there was a space that more than one person might lie down in.]

I thought I heard the people coming down from the bells; they all went out, and then it was so dark that I could not see my hand.

Well, I left this Bishop, and came out and fell upon my knees, and asked the Lord what I was to do first; and he said.

Get thy way up the bell-loft; I had never been there, and I went round and round; I had a sort of guess of the place from hearing the men as I thought come down; I then struck a light with a flint and a razor that I had got, and some tinder that I had brought from my landlord's.

I saw there were plenty of ropes -- then I cut one, and then another; but I had no idea they were so long, and I kept draw, draw, and the rope came up. I dare say I had hundred feet.

Well, thought I to myself, this will make a man-rope, a sort of scaling rope, and I tied knots in it.

Ay, that's it, I know it well enough (pointing to the rope which lay upon the table). So, I went down to the body of the cathedral, and bethought me how I should get inside.

I thought if I did so, by throwing the rope over the organ, I might set it ganging, and that would spoil the job.

So, I made an end of the rope fast, and went hand over-hand over the gates, and got down on the other side, and fell on *my knees and prayed to the Lord -- and he told me, that do what I would, they would take me.*

Then I asked the Lord what I was to do with velvet, and he told me, and I thought it would do for my hairy jacket, that I have at Lincoln.

I have a very good seal-skin one there. I wish I had it with me, that I might show it you.

Then I got all ready. Glory to God, I never felt so happy; but I had a hard night's work of it, particularly with a hungered belly.

Well, I got a bit of wax-candle, and I set fire to one heap, and with the matches I set fire to the other.

I then tied up the things that the Lord had given me for my hire, in this very handkerchief that I have in my hand.

[The prisoner then went on to describe his escape by means of the rope, nearly in the same terms as have been stated, and of his proceeding to Hexham; that on the road the coaches passed him, but he laid himself down, and was never seen.]

While I was at Hexham (I think I had been there two days) I had been to pray with a poor woman, and the Hexham man came and tipped me on the shoulder." He concluded by saying, "I's tired, or I'd tell you more."

The unfortunate man was ordered to be detained during his Majesty's pleasure, and was afterwards conveyed to a lunatic asylum.

It appeared that this maniac was the brother of the painter, who, for his magnificent productions, has attained so much celebrity.

Up to the time of this transaction, he had gained a precarious livelihood by hawking books; having been, however, as we have before stated, once or twice confined in a mad-house.

It is very remarkable that York Minster has repeatedly suffered from fire. Its origin may be dated from A.D. 626. In 741 it was dreadfully damaged by fire, and remained in that state till 767, when it was taken down, rebuilt, and completed, and was consecrated in 780.

Thus, it stood until 1069, when the Northumbrians, aided by the Danes, having besieged the city of York, the garrison set fire to several houses in the suburbs, which fire unfortunately extended further than they intended, and, amongst other buildings, burnt the Minster to the ground.

In 1137, the same fire which burnt St. Mary's Abbey, St. Leonard's Hospital, thirty-nine churches in the city, and one in the suburbs, again destroyed the Minster; since which there had not been any damage done to it by fire, excepting two trifling occurrences, which have taken place through the neglect of the workmen, within the last sixty years, up to the time of Martin's mad attempt.

In the present year (1840), it has again suffered severely from an accidental conflagration, which has destroyed nearly the whole of that portion of the ancient building which the former catastrophe had left standing.

Richard Martin

Of the four brothers Richard is the least notorious.

Born in 1779 in Brig O'Doon, Ayrshire while his father was in America, he was initially apprenticed to Thomas Graham a carrier based in Hexham.

He did however go on to join the army initially with the Northumberland Fencibles. This regiment went on to be part of the Grenadier Guards and Richard did become a Grenadier Guard.

He served in the army for 22 years He is described as an expert soldier, he served in Ireland assisting to quell the Irish rebellion.

He went on to become a Quarter-Master Sergeant with the Guards and fought in Spain, Portugal (Peninsula War) and at Waterloo.

Remarkably he was never wounded.

I have a record that his wife was Mary and that they had at least one child Eliza Mary.

He died in 1836

Ann Martin

There is very little information widely available about Ann the only daughter to survive to adulthood. However, another researcher into the family did make contact with a John Adam who is descended from Ann through her daughter Isabella.

Fenwick and Isabella Martin are the fifth times Great Grandparents of John Adam, through Ann Martin and her daughter Isabella Ann.

Family sources state that Ann was the Sister of John Martin, the famous painter.

They also knew the date of her death, age at death and place of burial in Brompton cemetery.

Her husband was said to be John Atkinson but further research revealed he was in fact Thomas Atkinson.

A reminder: About 1776, Ann's grandparents Richard and Ann Thompson left East Land Ends and went to Scotland, in response to the Duke of Argyll's appeal to English farmers to teach husbandry to the Highlanders. They settled at Kilcolmcille on Kintyre.

Fenwick and Isabella followed and lived at the Brig of Doon, near Ayr, where their son Richard was born.

Ann was born in 1784 and by this time Isabella was living with her parents at Kilcolmcille.

Fenwick had left home and enlisted in the army at the height of the American War of Independence.

When Ann was born however it is recorded that Fenwick was back in England, giving fencing lessons at the Chancellor's Head on Newgate Street in Newcastle.

Fenwick, Isabella, Richard, the eldest child William and Ann eventually returned from Scotland to the cottage at East Land Ends, where John was born on 19th July 1789.

Ann's baptism took place on 24th July, in Southend, Argyllshire. The Southernmost village on Kintyre.

The family moved to Newcastle in 1803 and nothing more is known of Ann until her marriage to Thomas Atkinson, a Boot Maker, in April 1807 at St. John's Church, Newcastle.

Both Ann and Thomas were able to sign their names in the marriage register, unlike many others on the same page.

On 4th January 1809 a daughter Isabella Ann Atkinson was born and she was baptised on 26th February at Postern Street Independent, Newcastle.

According to family sources Isabella was their only child.

At some point Thomas Atkinson and Ann moved to London, probably to be close to John.

Ann's daughter Isabella married Henry Warren, probably about 1829, in London.

(Henry Warren became President of the Institute of Painters in Water Colours in 1839 a post he held until his resignation in 1873 at the age of 77 years. In 1839 he painted a portrait of John Martin which hung in the Royal Academy.)

Isabella and Henry's first son Albert Henry, was born on 5th May 1830 and all together Isabella and Henry presented Ann with nine grandchildren.

Three of the five girls died fairly young but the four boys all survived to become artists like their father.

In 1841 Ann Atkinson aged 50, was a lady of independent means living or staying at 7, Camera Square, Chelsea.

By 1851 she was living with her brother John, his wife Susan and their daughter Isabella and two servants, in Lindsay House, Chelsea.

Ann Atkinson (nee Martin), the widow of Thomas Atkinson Boot Maker, died of General Debility and Paralysis on 29th January 1867 'age 80 years' (she was probably 82) and was buried in the Brompton Cemetery in a grave with other members of the Warren family.

Ann, the only surviving girl of the Martin family, had outlived all her brothers.

Ann's daughter, Isabella Ann, became 'Dame Isabella' when Henry Warren was awarded the Order of Leopold in 1868.

(John Martin had been awarded this honour thirty-five years earlier).

Ann's daughter Isabella died in 1871.

John Martin

I have left the most famous member of the family till last as so much has been written about him over the years. Rather than taking bits and pieces from these other researchers it may be more interesting to hear his story in his own words.

The Illustrated London News had contained a review outlining the life of John Martin, written by his son in law Peter Cunningham. The article was not to John's liking and he set about to put the record straight.

The following autobiographical letter from the pen of the great artist and Haydonian was deemed so interesting it was reproduced in full by the editor of the famous publication, on March 17th 1849

MR. JOHN MARTIN   Lindsey House, Chelsea. March 14, 1849.

To the Editor of the ILLUSTRATED LONDON NEWS

Sir,—Your journal is so distinguished for the accuracy of its statements, as rarely to present occasion for question; but the article concerning me in your last number was so unfortunate a tissue of errors from beginning to end, that it can only have the effect of misleading your readers; and I must, therefore, request your insertion of the following particulars, which, however brief, may at least be relied on, and thus supersede the unauthorised sketches of my life which have hitherto appeared.

I was born at a house called the East Land Ends, Haydon Bridge, near Hexham, 19th July, 1789, and received the rudiments of my education at the well-known free-school of that place.

Having, from my earliest years, attempted to draw, and expressed a determination to "be a painter," the question arose "how to turn my desires to profitable account" and it was ultimately decided to make me a herald painter in consequence of which, upon the removal of my family to Newcastle, I was, when 14, apprenticed to Wilson, the coach builder, of that town.

I worked with him for a year, in no small degree disgusted at the drudgery which, as junior apprentice, I had to endure, and at not being allowed to practice the higher mysteries of the art when, just previously to the expiration of the year (from which period I was to have received an increase of pay), one of the senior apprentices told me that my employer would evade the payment of the first quarter, on the grounds that "I went on trial," but that "it was not in the indentures."

As it had been foretold, so it turned out. Upon claiming the increase, I was referred to my articles, and the original sum was tendered.

This I indignantly rejected, saying, "What! you're soon beginning then, and mean to serve me the same as you did such an one? but I won't submit;" and, turning on my heel, I hastened home.

My father highly approved of my conduct - declared that I should not go back - and immediately furnished me with proper drawing materials, the most satisfactory reward I could receive.

I worked away to my heart's content for some days; when, at length, while so employed the town sergeant came to take me off to the Guildhall, to answer charges brought against me by my master.

I was dreadfully frightened, the more so as none of my family was within call to accompany me: and, on entering the court, my heart sank at sight of the aldermen and my master, with lowering face, and his witnesses.

I was charged on oath with insolence - having run away - rebellious conduct and threatening to do a private injury.

In reply, I simply stated the facts as they occurred.

The witness produced against me proved the correctness of my statement in every particular and the consequence was a decision in my favour.

Turning then, to my master, I said; "You have stated your dissatisfaction with me, and apprehensions of my doing you a private injury: under these circumstances, you can have no objection to returning my indentures."

Mr. Wilson was not prepared for this, but the Alderman immediately said, "Yes Mr. Wilson, you must give the boy his indentures".

They were accordingly handed over to me; and I was so overjoyed that, without waiting longer, I bowed and thanked the court, and running off to the coach factory, flourished the indentures over my head, crying, "I've got my indentures, and your master has taken a false oath; and I don't know whether he is not in the pillory by this!"

My family were delighted with the spirit I had displayed, and at my emancipation from an occupation they saw was uncongenial, and my father at once took measures to place me under an Italian master of great merit, and some reputation in Newcastle, named Boniface Musso, the father of the celebrated enamel painter, Charles Muss.

I remained under his instructions about a year, when Mr. C. Muss, who was settled in London, wished his father to come and reside with him, and M. Musso urged upon my parents the advantage of my accompanying him.

After much cogitation, many misgivings on my mother's part, and solemn charges to our friend, it was ultimately agreed that I should join him in London within a few months.

I accordingly arrived in London at the beginning of September, 1806; but, unluckily for the lovers of romance, I was not cast upon the wide world in quite such a forlorn and destitute condition as your earlier contributor states; for I had a good outfit - small, though sufficient funds for immediate purposes, notwithstanding my having been robbed off all my loose cash, by a poor passenger in the ship - and most important of all, I was placed under the protection of kind and excellent friends.

The treatment I experienced from Mr. C. Muss soon satisfied me that he conceived my means to be far more extended than they were; I therefore took an early opportunity of informing him that I had resolved never more to receive pecuniary assistance from my parents, who had already done enough in providing means for establishing me in London; that, as my present resources were not equal to a due recompense for his liberality, I thought it only right to tell him my position.

He was pleased with my honourable candour, and saying that he would do all in his power to promote my laudable intentions, immediately undertook to employ me in his glass and china painting establishment in a department where my facility in designing and painting landscape scenes would be very useful; and from this time, I supported myself solely by my own exertions, and with advantage to my employers.

After a few months, feeling uncomfortable, owing to some little differences with a member of Mr. M's family, I removed from his house in Wynyatt Street, New River Head, to Adam Street West, Cumberland Place, continuing to work for Mr. Muss's firm during the day, and sitting up at night till two and three o'clock in the morning acquiring that knowledge of perspective and architecture which has since been so valuable to me.

Here I remained till 1809, when I married, and removed to Northumberland Street, Marylebone, thence to High Street; thence, in 1818, to 30, Allsop Terrace, New Road; and thence, after 30 years' residence, to my present abode; and these are the only places in London I have ever lived in.

Shortly before my marriage Mr. Muss's establishment broke up, and those employed in it had the option of seeking independent employment or following the fortunes of the different members of the firm.

I, of course, accompanied my friend, and was subsequently engaged with him in the glass painting, carried on by Mr. Collins, in the Strand, occupying my evenings upon water-colour drawings, and contriving, in odd hours, to paint in oil my first picture ever exhibited ("A Clytie"), which was sent to the Academy in 1810, and rejected for want of room, though not condemned, as I afterwards learnt through Mr. Tresham.

I therefore sent it again in 1811, when it was hung in a good situation in the Great Room!

At the beginning of the following year, having now lost my employment at Collins's, it became indeed necessary to work hard, and, as I was ambitious of fame, I determined on painting a large picture, "Sadak," which was executed in a month.

You may easily guess my feelings when I overheard the men who were placing it in the frame disputing as to which was the top of the picture!

The work, however, though hung in the ante-room of the Royal Academy, received, to my inexpressible delight, a notice in the newspapers, and was eventually sold, under interesting circumstances, to the late Mr. Manning, for 50 guineas.

The following year, 1813, I sent "The Expulsion" to the British Institution, and "Adam's first sight of Eve," to the Royal Academy, and was again given a place in the Great Room.

My next painting, "Clytie," though a picture which has stood the test of criticism during many years, was in 1814 placed in the ante-room of the Royal Academy.

The following year I sent the "Joshua," which was again hidden in the ante room; the next year, 1817, I sent it to the British Institution, where it attracted great attention, and I was rewarded with the chief premium of the year, £100; but the picture was not sold till some years afterwards, when it went as a companion to the "Belshazzar."

Down to this period I had supported myself and family by pursuing almost every branch of my profession - teaching - painting small oil pictures, glass enamel paintings, watercolour drawings; in fact, the usual tale of a struggling artist's life.

I had been so successful with my sepia drawings that the Bishop of Salisbury, the tutor to the Princess Charlotte, advised me not to risk my reputation by attempting the large picture of "Joshua."

As is generally the case in such matters, these well-meant recommendations had no effect; but, at all events, the confidence I had in my powers was justified, for the success of my "Joshua" opened a new era to me.

In 1818 I removed to a superior house, and had to devote my time mainly to executing some immediately profitable works; but, in 1819, I produced the "Fall of Babylon," which was second only to the "Belshazzar" in the attention it excited.

The following year came "Macbeth," one of my most successful landscapes.

Then, in 1821, "Belshazzar's Feast," an elaborate picture, which occupied a year in executing, and which received the premium of £200 from the British Institution.

In the next year, 1822, appeared the "Destruction of Herculaneum," another elaborate work.

In 1823, the "Seventh Plague" and "Paphian Bower."

In 1824 the "Creation;" in 1826 the "Deluge," and in 1828 the "Fall of Nineveh,"

In addition to the above were many smaller pictures, duplicates of some of the above subjects, sketches, and drawings, but the most important of all was my acquiring the art of engraving, and producing the "Illustrations of Milton," designed on the plates (and for which I received 2000 guineas) the "Belshazzar's Feast," the first large steel plate ever engraved in mezzotinto; the "Joshua" and the "Deluge," between the years 1823 and 1828.

Thus it will be seen that all my greatest works which have gained me a reputation both at home and abroad, were produced within the eleven years immediately succeeding the first fair exhibition of my "Joshua," and that "the bitter sayings of envious artists" arose from no inertness on my part, whilst the rapid and substantial success which attended my efforts certainly warranted no supposition of any "false and temporary appreciation of my merits."

On the contrary, the inferences are all the other way, if we may judge from the fact that, of all my numerous works, I have but one oil painting in my own possession - the earlier works having been purchased by the late Mr. Henry Phillip Hope, the Duke of Buckingham, Lord de Tabley, Earl of Durham, Earl Grey, and others; the more recent ones by the Duke of Sutherland, Prince Albert, and Mr. Scarisbrick - to whose cultivated taste I am as much indebted as to his liberal patronage.

The notice and honours I have received from foreign courts arose chiefly from the circulation of my engravings, as only two of my pictures have ever been seen abroad - the "Fall of Nineveh" at Brussels, and the "Deluge" in Paris; the first procured me the large medal of the Exhibition, the order of Leopold, and my election as a member of the Academy of Antwerp; the second the gold medal, and a magnificent present of Sevres from the King of the French.

These facts show that if I had enemies among the artists, their aspersions did not retard my progress, However, I myself much doubt the existence of such ill-feeling in the outset, though there can be little question that eventually my success, by my own independent means, raised a sufficient number of detractors.

As regards the Royal Academy, I, doubtless, had reason to complain; for as I progressed in art and reputation my places on its walls retrograded my first works being placed in the Great Room, whereas, all the subsequent, and with every show of probability, superior, productions were placed in a dark hole called the Ante-room.

This led to my ceasing to enter my name upon its books, to my considering its laws, and to my opposition on public grounds, my quarrel being, not with individual members, but with the association itself; for I was satisfied that a body so constituted, a close and narrow monopoly, with the privileges of a Royal charter and power of a public institution, could not but produce a mischievous effect on art itself.

I have expressed these convictions in evidence before the House of Commons, and yet hope to see a thorough reform, and all such monopolies thrown open.

I have already encroached so much upon your space that I have scarcely room to account for the last 20 years of my life; suffice it, that some portion was devoted to engraving, which I was eventually obliged to abandon, owing to the imperfect laws of copyright, my property being constantly and variously infringed, that it became ruinous to contend with those who robbed me and I was, therefore, driven from the market by inferior copies of my own works, to the manifest injury of my credit and pecuniary resources, while I may, without vanity, affirm that even art itself suffers by the noncirculation of the engravings, for, of course, neither my own plates nor the pirated copies will sell without the impulse of novelty.

In consequence of the strong interest I had always felt in the improvement of the condition of the people, and the sanitary state of the country, I turned my attention to engineering subjects; and two-thirds of my time, and a very large portion of my pecuniary means, have, since 1821, been devoted to the objects I had at heart, though even here I have been obstructed and injured by the same objection of the inefficiency of the patent laws, and, indeed, total absence of real protection of original designs in engineering and mechanics.

Your limits will not admit of the particulars of injuries I have sustained on this head, and I will therefore merely enumerate the plans I have put forth.

My attention was first occupied in endeavouring to procure an improved supply of pure water to London, diverting the sewage from the river, and rendering it available as manure; and in 1827 and 1828 I published plans for the purpose.

In 1829 I published further plans for accomplishing the same objects by different means, namely, a weir across the Thames, and for draining the marshy lands, &c. In 1832, 1834, 1836, 1838, 1842, 1843, 1845, and 1847, I published and republished additional particulars - being so bent upon my object that I was determined never to abandon it; and though I have reaped no other advantage I have, at least, the satisfaction of knowing that the agitation thus kept up constantly, solely by myself, has resulted in a vast alteration in the quantity and quality of water supplied by the companies, and in the establishment of a Board of Health, which will, in all probability, eventually carry out most of the objects I have been so long urging.

Amongst the other proposals which I have advanced is my railway connecting the river and docks with all the railways that diverge from London, and apparently approved by the Railway Termini Commissioners, as the line they intimate coincides with that submitted by me, and published in their report - the principle of rail adopted by the Great Western line - the lighthouse for the sands appropriated by Mr. Walker In his Maplin sand lighthouse - the flat anchor and wire cable - mode of ventilating coal mines - floating harbour and pier - iron ship - and various other inventions of comparatively minor importance, but all conducing to the great ends of improving the health of the country, increasing the produce of the land, and furnishing employment for the people in remunerative works.

With every apology for the length of my communication, which must satisfy you that I have never been an idle man,

I remain, sir,

your obedient servant,

JOHN MARTIN.

Thomas Bell & Be-Ro Flour

Many people don't realise that the famous Be- Ro Flour has its origins in Longhorsley in Northumberland. The story in brief generally told is that Thomas's mother Ann was left widowed when her husband William died when the children were small so she had to run a small bakery to keep the family alive.

There is certainly truth within the story however you should realise that the Bell family had long held the land West Moor in the Freeholder Quarter of Long Horsley and that his wife Ann of the Lilburn family also came from a family of landowners and farmers.

While there is no doubt, they had to work hard it is wrong to paint the picture that they were in any way destitute. Indeed, in the 1841 census taken just a year after William and Ann Lilburn had married, William is described as being of independent means.

He died in 1854 and in 1861 Ann is described as a landed proprietor.

The family ran the Longhorsley village grocery shop at 1 South Road, it lay to the west of the main road and is the building most recently remembered as housing the Post Office.

In the course of helping his mother young Thomas began playing with various rising agents in flour.

His development however was not the world's first self-raising flour, that title goes to Henry Jones from Bristol who obtained a patent in 1851 when Thomas was only three years old. It is fair however to describe Thomas' creation as the most successful.

In 1875 Ann bought two old cottages across the road from the shop, she had them pulled down and with her daughter also Ann she built a house and shop and upstairs she created the original Longhorsley Mission a religious meeting room, initially called Longhorsley Hall it was renamed Belmont.

A few years earlier Thomas had decided to take his new self-raising flour business to Newcastle and more specifically the Groat Market in the yard of the Blackie Boy Pub. He called his business Bells Royal Works and the product was initially Bells Royal Flour.

The business subsequently moved to Low Friar Street and from there to Bath Lane

The Be-Ro Website states that the name changed after the death of King Edward VII when restrictions were made on companies using the word Royal as a trade or registered name. In fact, that is incorrect King Edward VII died in 1910 whereas the name Be-Ro had been used since about 1896 and Thomas had it patented as the company name in 1906.

The main reason was that there was an American product called Royals Baking Powder and Thomas felt the names were too similar, his wife actually chose the new name.

His wife was Mary J Stephenson the daughter of Isaac who was an engine driver, Thomas and Mary married in the last quarter of 1870 and initially lived with her family at 25 Milton Street, Newcastle. In 1871 Thomas described himself as a grocer.

In 1881 Thomas and Mary lived at 15 Choppington Street, Newcastle with three children. By 1891 they had moved to 72 Brighton Grove, Newcastle, there were now 6 children and a servant.

By the 1901 census Thomas was describing himself as a wholesale grocer and an employer, the family had now moved to 154 Marine Avenue, Monkseaton.

He died on 22nd February 1925. His son Robert continued running the business and it expanded via Carlisle, Leeds, Edinburgh, Sheffield, Birmingham and Nottingham.

In 1958 the business was bought by Rank-Hovis Ltd

The famous books had been introduced in the 1920s. In the early 1920s, the most commonly used type of flour was plain flour. Self-raising flour was more expensive and considered a novelty - consumers bought plain flour direct from the miller and self-raising flour was only sold into independent grocers.

In a bid to make self-raising flour more popular among the general public, the company staged a series of exhibitions in the early 1920s where freshly baked scones, pastries and cakes were sold for a shilling to visitors. These were so popular that people demanded to have copies of the recipes so that they could bake the dishes at home.

Plasticine and North Shields

In 2009 North Tyneside Council erected street furniture to resemble plasticine shapes and colours. Sadly by 2011 these had been removed because of complaints from the public as the design of the seats include a dip and when it rained this dip retained the water for several days making the seats unusable. The seats were repainted to various colours and designs and relocated elsewhere within the region including a local sixth form college.

But why did the council involve themselves in commemorating plasticine in the first place? It was because William Harbutt the creator of plasticine had been North Shields born.

William Harbutt was the one of eight children of Thomas and Elizabeth Harbutt (nee Jeffcoate).

The 1841 census shows that Thomas lived in Monkseaton and was admitted to the St Georges Lodge of Freemasonry later that year. He seems to have been a man of substance as in 1834 he appears as a voter owning a property in Church Way Tynemouth.

In 1842 he left Monkseaton and his neighbours laid on a farewell party for him at the Ship Inn, Monkseaton the home of John Duxfield on the 10th March that year. Tickets were sold for this event at the price of 2s 6d each. In modern terms that would be £12.50 per ticket.

Tomlinson describes a farmhouse of Thomas Mills built in 1688. It had a carved fireplace with a stucco frieze bearing the coat of arms of Charles II, with the monogram 'CR' and the Stuart motto "Beati Pacifici" (blessed are the peacemakers). The building became **The Ship Inn** *in 1790, but was destroyed by fire in 1923. The coat of arms was rescued and is now in the Urban District Council Chambers at Whitley Bay. The inn was rebuilt on a site slightly to the* *west. This was one of a number of fine 17th century houses in Monkseaton. To the west of The Ship was another farmhouse with a fine 17th century fireplace. There was a cottage in 1683 at the east end of the village and in 1698 Red House Farm is recorded.*

At that time Thomas was described as a spirit merchant and a trustee of Monkseaton Brewery and at the farewell dinner Thomas was presented with a silver cream jug bought from a collection by the workmen at the brewery. In 1914 the brewery closed and the Monkseaton Arms now stands on the site but an old wall is a remnant of the brewery which was a successor to an older brewery created by monks in medieval times.

As stated above Thomas and Elizabeth had eight children in total: Thomas Jeffcoate Harbutt who firstly married Elizabeth Leslie but after her death in 1864 he sold his ironmongery business and subsequently married Annabelle Jennings. For a while they lived in Jersey with children from both of his marriages but later, they moved initially to Australia and from there to New Zealand.

Thomas Jeffcoate Harbutt

The next child was Mary Jane Harbutt, she married William Markus a master printer, they too settled in Jersey before moving back to England William was a bookseller while in Jersey.

Ann Harbutt married John Dawson who was a newspaper proprietor from Skipton, he owned the Craven Pioneer a liberal weekly paper and was also senior partner in Edmonson & Co, a publisher. Their son William went on to write "A History of Skipton".

Elizabeth Whitehouse Harbutt married John Holliday the son of a solicitor's Managing Clerk. John set up an Iron Galvanising and Chain Manufacturer and so in time became a rival to his father in law, Thomas.

Hannah married Robert Atkin and nothing much more is known of them.

Margaret remained unmarried until her death in Bristol in 1932

Sarah died when she was just 1 year old.

That leaves William the hero of this account, born 13th February 1844 in North Shields, his earliest home was 63 Bedford Street. William was named after his uncle, his father's only brother a missionary in Samoa, William by 1861 moved to Jersey and worked for his brother in law William Markus as a bookseller's assistant.

An accident when he was young had left him with a limp which was with him throughout his life.

After that initial working start as bookseller's assistant in 1869 he began studying art at the National Art Training School (now known as the Royal College of Art) in South Kensington, the qualification he gained when he left in 1873 enabled him to describe himself as Associate of Royal College of Art (A.R.C.A) in the 1890s when the college was renamed. He was qualified to teach elementary and architectural drawing,

After he gained his qualification he taught at first as a freehand drawing master at Somersetshire College at 11 The Circus, Bath which had once been home to William Pitt the elder. Alexander Graham Bell, the inventor of the telephone taught there for one year in 1866

In 1874 he became the Headmaster of the Bath School of Art & Design, a disagreement with the ruling committee led him to leave in 1877 and with his wife Elizabeth (Bessie) Cambridge set up his own school the Paragon Art Studio just yards from his former employer. One of his students was his own nephew Robert Barkas Dawson from Skipton.

Robert Barkas Dawson (1863-?) married Bessie Lord (1859-1923). Robert was an art teacher and headmaster and the

brother of William Harbutt Dawson. Among their children was Kathleen Anne Dawson (1894-1992). Kathleen studied art and became a watercolourist. In 1919 she married Ronald Nesbitt Hawes (1895-1969). Ronald served in the army in both world wars, reaching the rank of Brigadier. He also served as a diplomat in Burma and in 1948 he was knighted for his service. And somewhere along the line added a hyphen.

Kathleen died in Australia.

Bessie, whom William had married on 8th August 1876, was a noted artist in her own right specialising in miniatures and was commissioned by Queen Victoria to paint portraits of the Queen and the late Prince Albert. They were originally hung at Frogmore, Windsor and more recently have been displayed at the Victoria art Gallery, Bath.

The couple settled at Hartley House, Belvedere, Lansdown, Bath and it was there that William began experimenting with clay as he had found that the clay used by students was messy and dried too quickly.

Using a makeshift laboratory in the basement William began experimenting with various measures of calcium carbonate, petroleum jelly, stearic acid, various aliphatic acids, whiting and perfume.

Eventually he produced a non-toxic, sterile, soft and malleable clay which did not dry out on being exposed to the air. The final mix was bulking agent principally gypsum, petroleum jelly, lime, lanolin and stearic acid. This was the birth of plasticine

He obtained his first patent in 1897 and after a period of home experimentation production began out of an old flour mill at the Grange, High Street, Bathampton.

As an employer he seems to have been everything an employee could want. He arranged annual outings often involving bussing the entire workforce and their families for a steamship cruise along the Thames.

He encouraged ball games at lunch time often extending the lunch break if a score needed to be determined. If the weather was exceptionally warm, he wasn't averse to sending the staff home early.

In the winter if the water had frozen, he encouraged skating at lunch time on the frozen Kennet and Avon Canal which ran beside the factory.

Plasticine began as a modelling material for art students and was originally produced as a grey product but when he moved on to supply in a range of colours it quickly became apparent that it also made an excellent toy for children. He wrote a number of books and pamphlets to explain the product and how it could be used

Meanwhile William was also active in local politics, he was a district and a parish councillor and stood for election to Somerset County Council.

He and Elizabeth had seven children:

Noel Cambridge William Harbutt 1877-1949

Olive Cambridge Harbutt 1878-1965

Ruby Cambridge Harbutt 1880-1880

Beryl Cambridge Harbutt 1883-1977

Eric Jefcoate Cambridge Harbutt 1884-1969

Enid Cambridge Harbutt 1886-1973

Owen Cambridge Harbutt 1889-1993

In 1914 plasticine took a new turn when William applied for a patent for what he described as an improved plasticine composition. The plan was to take basic plasticine and work it into a quantity of lamb's wool or cotton wool in a fairly divided state until a practically homogeneous mass is obtained.

The provisional specification goes on to say "This improved plastic composition when rolled into thin sheets is applicable to a variety of surgical and other uses as for bandages. It forms a very efficient ear stopping for gunners to prevent gun deafness in ship turrets and forts and for boilermakers using pneumatic percussion tools. It is also applicable in the resetting of broken and fractured limbs and for malformed joints in which case a layer is applied to the limb before the usual plaster case is made and, in many cases making the use of plaster of paris unnecessary."

It seems that the development was used as ear plugs during the war but I have not found any application of the other suggestions. That is unfortunate as some 70 years later a number of employees of shipbuilders successfully took action against various shipbuilders for hearing loss where adequate ear protection had not been provided.

During World War II, Plasticine was used by bomb disposal officer Major John P. Hudson R.E. as part of the defusing process for the new German "Type Y" battery-powered bomb fuse. The "Type Y" fuse has an anti-disturbance device that had to be disabled before the fuse could be removed. Plasticine was used to build a dam around the head of the fuse to hold some liquid oxygen. The liquid oxygen cooled the battery down to a temperature at which it would no longer function; with the battery out of commission, the fuse could be removed safely.

William made many overseas trips, notably USA, Australia and New Zealand. On one of those trips to the USA he died of pneumonia in New York in 1921. His body was brought back to England for burial.

His descendants continued to run Harbutts Plasticine Ltd. In 1957 the factory was totally destroyed by fire as described below in the appeal action.

Harbutt's "Plasticine" Ltd v Wayne Tank and Pump Co Ltd 1970

Harbutts engaged Wayne Tank & Pump to design and install in their factory, an old mill, a pipe system to convey hot molten wax used in the production of Plasticine. Wayne Tank unwisely chose to use plastic piping. Once installed, Wayne Tank chose to initiate the new system at night, but without any supervision. The system had a faulty thermostat and molten wax overheated. The plastic pipes melted and the molten wax escaped and caught fire, causing a huge conflagration. By the morning, the entire factory was destroyed. This led to one of the biggest-ever claims for damages in England. Wayne Tank sought to rely on a clause in the contract that purported to limit their liability for breach of contract.

The company was sold in due course and since 1963 the product has been manufactured in Thailand.

The Wooden Dollies of North Shields

The Wooden Dollies are fairly well known to most visitors to North Shields but not so many people know their history.

To trace the origin of the tradition we need to travel back in time to a christening on the 11th February 1756 of David Bartleman the son of Alexander Bartleman and his wife Margaret nee Murray, David was one of four children of the couple. It is worth mentioning that David's older brother Alexander had a son in 1803 also called Alexander who, in 1851 became mayor of Tynemouth. In addition, he ran Northumberland Brewery which was to later merge and become Bartleman and Creighton Brewery.

Returning however to Alexander and Margaret, assisted by his wife Alexander senior was both a brewer and a shipbuilder and one ship built was a coal brig called appropriately The Alexander & Margaret. Like many ships of the era the ship had a figurehead, this was in the form of a woman and was supposed to denote good luck. The figure has been described as: *'no slim, simpering, Goddess-looking creature, but a bluff, saucy, hearty-looking hussy, with a full flaunting petticoat something in the style of good Queen Bess."*

This ship in January1781 was captained by the above-mentioned son David and was sailing of the Norfolk Coast.

Also, at sea was a notorious pirate and privateer who went by various first names William, Daniel and John, his surname however was always constant, that was Fall.

At this time the American War of Independence was ongoing and it should be remembered that France had aligned themselves with the Americans in this war.

Fall held a Letter of Marque from America. This document authorized the captain to capture enemy ships, their crews, and their cargoes. Falls practice was to demand a ransom from the Captain and, once paid he would allow the ship to travel freely.

The Alexander and Margaret had a crew of ten men and boys, it carried only light armaments amounting to 3 pounder cannons, this was one of the smallest cannons in existence.

On the 31st January Bartleman's ship came under attack off the Norfolk coast from Falls Cutter "Fearnought", the cutter carried a crew of nearly one hundred and was armed with 18 x 4 pounder cannons. Miraculously the much smaller coal brig managed to fight off the attack and make its escape.

Two hours later however Falls privateer again launched an attack, this attack was far more ferocious and Daniel McAuley, the mate was badly injured and died from loss of blood. Daniel too was seriously injured and obliged to yield to Captain Fall, the ransom was 400 guineas, which, in modern terms equates to about £72,000.

Having paid the ransom, the ship limped into Great Yarmouth but David died of his wounds just two weeks later on 14th February aged just 25.

Alexander had the following memorial erected over his son's grave

> **A Memorial in Yarmouth Churchyard   Recorded in 1806**
>
> TO THE MEMORY OF **DAVID BARTLEMAN** MASTER OF THE BRIG "**ALEXANDER AND MARGARET**" OF NORTH SHIELDS
> WHO ON THE 31ST DAY OF JANUARY 1781 ON THE NORFOLK COAST WITH ONLY 3 THREE POUNDERS AND TEN MEN AND BOYS NOBLY DEFENDED HIMSELF AGAINST A CUTTER CARRYING 18 FOUR POUNDERS AND UPWARDS OF A HUNDRED MEN COMMANDED BY THE NOTORIOUS ENGLISH PIRATE "FALL" AND FAIRLY BEAT HIM OFF.
>
> TWO HOURS AFTER THE ENEMY CAME DOWN UPON HIM AGAIN WHEN TOTALLY DISABLED HIS MATE **DANIEL MAC AULEY** EXPIRING WITH LOSS OF BLOOD AND HIMSELF DANGEROUSLY WOUNDED HE WAS OBLIGED TO STRIKE AND RANSOM. HE BROUGHT HIS SHATTERED VESSEL INTO YARMOUTH WITH MORE THAN THE HONOUR OF A CONQUERER AND DIED HERE IN CONSEQUENCE OF HIS WOUNDS ON THE FOURTEENTH OF FEBRUARY FOLLOWING IN THE TWENTYFITH YEAR OF HIS AGE.
>
> TO COMMEMORATE THE GALLENTRY OF HIS SON,THE BRAVERY OF HIS FAITHFUL MATE AND AT THE SAME TIME MARK THE INFAMY OF A SAVAGE PIRATE HIS AFFLICTED FATHER **ALEXANDER BARTLEMAN** HAS ORDERED THIS STONE TO BE ERECTED OVER HIS HONOURABLE GRAVE.
>
> T'WAS GREAT HIS FOE
> THOUGH STRONG WAS INFAMOUS
> THE FOE OF HUMANKIND
> A MANLY INDIGNATION FIRED HIS BREATH
> THANK GOD MY SON HAS DONE HIS DUTY.
>
> A TOMBSTONE IN ST NICHOLAS CHURCHYARD,GREAT YARMOUTH

Two hundred and thirty years after his death a family called Pearce, who believed that their ancestors had been pirates paid for the restoration and repositioning of the gravestone in St Nicholas Churchyard, Great Yarmouth.

Meanwhile Alexander had recovered the wooden dolly from the ship and had it transported back to his home at 23 Front Street, Tynemouth where he stood it in the front garden. The property no longer has a front garden and is home to "The Wine Chambers".

In 1814 the dolly was moved to a position on the Custom House Quay, Low Street, North Shields. This was the first of what has been to date seven "wooden" dollies.

It was situated in one of the busiest places at the time of North Shields. All of the adjacent buildings were involved in trade of one form or another, there were no less than 50 public houses, dance houses, coffee houses, chandlers and ropemakers in the vicinity. The dolly was used to haul spars and wood from the quay using rope wrapped around her.

Seamen took to cutting chunks off her as good luck charms on their subsequent voyages. This custom led to local urchins also hacking away at her and eventually a group of drunks pulled her out of the ground and cut off her head. This was in 1850.

This of course was a year before David's nephew became mayor and one has to assume that he already carried some influence.

What is certain is that a new dolly was quickly constructed to replace the first, built by a sailmaker called Hare.

She had a shorter life than her sister and just 14 years later she too was replaced on the 22nd June 1864, the day before the laying of the foundation stone for the new Low Lights Dock. This Dolly had previously been attached to the barque "Expert"

*A **barque**, **barc**, or **bark** is a type of sailing vessel with three or more masts having the fore and mainmasts rigged square and only the mizzen (the aft-most mast) rigged fore and aft.*

She too was attacked and chipped away. Her nose was totally hacked off and replaced with an iron one by local blacksmith Robert Pow. Sailors then began drilling holes in coins and nailing the coins to the dolly. This dolly was replaced in 1901, however that was not the end of her. In the 1930's she appeared in an antique shop in Newcastle after the owner a Mr Seery had bought her from a fisherman's widow. She was subsequently bought by a Dane and it is believed that she now resides in a Denmark Museum.

The 4th Wooden Dolly from 1902 was carved by May Spence of North Shields, this dolly did not resemble the previous effigies but was more in line with the typical image of a Cullercoats fishwife with shawl and creel on her back

New Wooden Dolly, North Shields.

The unveiling of this dolly included a procession with band and speeches. Inevitably she too was vandalised for souvenirs and good luck charms, her right elbow found its way to an hotel in Melbourne, Australia and the rest of her remains were found in a Whitby Breakers Yard. She was removed in 1957.

In 1958 the fifth wooden dolly was created by Robert Thompson Ltd in Kilburn; North Yorkshire and it had incorporated into the figure two mice as was the tradition with that company. Mahogany was used to create this figure.

This particular figure still stands but unlike her sisters for a long time she graced Northumberland Square but recently to protect her from vandalism has been moved into the adjacent library

The other end of North Shields however was not to be denied its dolly and an additional one was erected beside the Prince of Wales Pub formerly called The Wooden Dolly on the original Custom House Quay site, this is still there and is a larger copy of the 3rd dolly.

The most recent dolly is in fact only half a dolly as her body is only from the waist up. It was installed in 1993 at the one-time Wooden Doll pub formerly The King's Head and now called "How Do You Do" overlooking the Fish Quay, although referred to as a wooden dolly it is in fact made of clay and cast in plaster.

So, a pirate in the 18th century is responsible for seven different wooden dollies three of which still exist

Mawson Swan & Morgan

Most people recognise the name of Sir Joseph Wilson Swan as being the inventor of the electric lamp although a dispute over copyright with Thomas Edison did cast some doubt over who was first. Eventually the matter was resolved with a merger of Swan Electric Light Company and Edison Electric Light Company which was then renamed the Edison & Swan Electric Light Company commonly referred to as Ediswan in 1883.

Fewer people however are aware of his involvement in Bookseller Mawson Swan and Morgan.

Joseph Swan had twelve brothers and sisters and his eldest sibling was Elizabeth who had been born the same year as their parents John and Isabella had married in 1822.

It is worth commenting on the fact that the Swan family were descended from and related to the Swann farming family of Bedlington and Miss Mary Anne Swann a 72-year-old distant cousin was viciously murdered at her home Hirst Head Cottage in 1906 by a local man recently released from an asylum. The full story can be read on the internet at http://www.sixtownships.org.uk/hirst-head-farm-murder.html

Isabella had been born Isabella Cameron and she had a younger sister Jane born 1814.

Jane married a John Mawson a man born in Penrith in 1816 who sadly had a number of failed businesses behind him

John Mawson.

An early account of his business turnaround is as follows

John Mawson, a native of Penrith, was apprenticed to a chemist and druggist in Sunderland. When he had finished his apprenticeship, he began business on his own account in that borough, but was not successful. He shortly afterwards removed to Newcastle, where he opened a shop, and here he also failed. This failure, however, was due to his having stood bond to a large amount for a friend, who left Mr. Mawson to pay the money. Nothing daunted, he tried business once more, this time in Mosley Street, where he remained till his death. Here he was more fortunate, and began to make fight against his debts, having resolved to pay everybody to the last farthing. He himself said "I shall be eighty before I can pay all that I owe" He stoutly refused to take "the benefit of the Act," and, like most men who stick to a good resolution, he ultimately achieved his purpose. And he deserved to succeed, for he worked with great energy and determination. His first successful venture was the introduction into Newcastle of Rothwell's Fire Fuel, which he afterwards got a patent to manufacture. With this material he did a very large trade. His next venture was in German yeast, which was first imported into the North of England by Mr. Mawson. The writer remembers the crowds of people who used to go to his shop for this indispensable commodity, as that was the only place in the town where it could then be purchased.

By 1849 he had repaid his debts in full and indeed his grateful creditors then rewarded him with a bookcase containing many valuable books

In around 1844 his nephew by marriage, Joseph had begun working with him as is evidenced by this 1864 announcement

1864 Joseph Swan became a partner in the firm. 'CHEMICAL AND PHOTOGRAPHIC ESTABLISHMENT, 9 AND 13, MOSLEY STREET, NEWCASTLE-UPON-TYNE. JOHN MAWSON has much pleasure announcing to his Friends and Customers that he has taken into Partnership his Brother-in-Law, Mr. JOSEPH WILSON SWAN, who has been with him in his Business for nearly Twenty years. This Business in future, in all its Branches, will be carried on under the Style of MAWSON AND SWAN. JOHN MAWSON takes this opportunity expressing his Thanks to his Friends for the Favours conferred upon during the Twenty-five Years he has been engaged in business, and hopes to receive himself and Partner a continuance of their Support. January 1, 1864.'

You will notice that this announcement refers to Joseph as being his brother in law while I stated above that Joseph was his nephew. In fact, both statements are true. Jane the wife of John and aunt of Joseph had died of a serious illness. She was only thirty years old and left behind her 5-year-old daughter Lydia, a second daughter had died in infancy.

In 1848 John married his late wife's niece and Joseph's older sister Elizabeth.

John Mawson's standing in Newcastle grew enormously and he was elected to Newcastle Town Council for the All Saints ward in 1858. He was a member of the Peace Society and argued extensively for the abolition of slavery.

He has been described as: *Honest in business, intelligent as a politician, earnest in public matters, faithful at all timers to his convictions, Mr Mawson was certainly one of the most esteemed citizens of Newcastle. The integrity of his conduct, the excellence of his public, the spotless purity of his private life, and the tragic manner of his death, all conspire to claim for John Mawson a distinguished place in the catalogue of Newcastle worthies*,

Indeed, his death was tragic and looking back almost certainly avoidable.

In 1867 Mawson was sheriff of Newcastle.

On 17th December 1867 it was found that a considerable quantity of nitro-glycerine (use for blasting in mines) had been stored in nine tins or canisters in the cellar of The White Swan Yard, Cloth Market.

Following discussions with the Town Surveyor Thomas Bryson and magistrates an order was issued that it should removed out of the town.

The railway company refused to move it, so John Mawson as sheriff and Thomas Bryson decided that it should be transported by cart to the Town Moor and an area was identified where there was subsidence caused by the workings of the Spital Tongues Colliery.

On arrival at the moor the intention was to uncork the canisters and pour the material into the subsidence area. This was done but three of the canisters still felt weighty. Mawson ordered the workmen to use their shovels to take off the ends of the canisters and it was found that the material had crystallised.

Mawson ordered that soil be placed over the area where the nitro-glycerine had been poured and ordered that the three canisters which contained the crystallisation should be removed to a nearby hill for burial. He was one of those who was involved in removing the three canisters, the others were Thomas Bryson the before mentioned Town Surveyor, P.C. Donald Pain, James Shotton an employee of Mr Turnbull of White House Yard, Thomas Appleby, George Smith Stonehouse, Samuel Bell Wadley and an unidentified man.

Nobody is sure precisely what happened (it is thought that one of the canisters may have been dropped) but those left covering the area of subsidence reported a load explosion, the ground shaking and fragments of clothing and other items flying through the air.

On investigation various mutilated bodies were found, Mawson and Bryson were both still alive but died the following night in the Infirmary.

Although very keen on developing the photography side of the business it did commence as a chemist and druggist. It also supplied yeast and heavy oil. Indeed, the official description states that the business compounded and dispensed tinctures and essences and in the 1850s expanded into the manufacture of photographic collodion (the chemicals used in wet plate photography.)

Mawson's sudden death led to his widow and Joseph Swan's sister Elizabeth joining the board of the business.

The business expanded and diversified with the purchase of Joseph Marston's book and private lending library. Joseph Marston was also a chemist Ironically it is they book selling business for which Mawson Swan and Morgan is best remembered.

In around 1873 Thomas Morgan arrived in Newcastle from Belfast. He became involved with the business and was a welcome addition as Elizabeth preferred to be a sleeping partner and Joseph Swan had so many other projects in motion that he was little involved in the day to day running of the business.

Thomas therefore became a major asset to the ongoing success of the business.

By 1878 the business had been renamed Mawson Swan and Morgan.

Under Morgan's guidance the business flourished, he increased the departments adding stationary, a fine art gallery, artists equipment, leather goods, he increased the bookselling side of the business and introduced a printing division.

Courtesy of Tyne & Wear Archives Museum when the business was situated in Grainger Street, Newcastle upon Tyne

Meanwhile the chemist side of the business merged with a long-established chemist Proctor Son & Clague (John Proctor had set up an apothecary business in Newcastle in 1768) the new business became Mawson & Proctor.

Meanwhile Joseph Swan had been busy with his other projects, while working with wet photographic plates he had noticed that the heat increased the sensitivity of the silver bromide emulsion. By 1871 he had devised a method of drying the wet plates so making photography more convenient. In 1879 he patented bromide paper the paper commonly used in modern photographic prints.

He had as early as 1860 devised an early light bulb using carbonised paper ion an evacuated glass bulb however the lack of good vacuum resulted in too short a life span for the bulb and insufficient light.

This however did not discourage him and on 20th October 1880 a lecture was held at the Literary & Philosophical Hall.

At that time a Colonel Rookes Evelyn Bell Crompton had already built an arc lighting system and had also devised the Crompton Lamp. Swan sent Thomas Morgan to London to invite Colonel Crompton and escort him to this lecture.

The lecture was chaired by Sir William Armstrong the engineer. The 70 gas jets lighting the room were dimmed and 20 light bulbs were turned on. This was the first time in

Europe that a public building had been illuminated with incandescent lamps.

Colonel Crompton went on to build Swans lamp under licence and his company dominated the British lighting market.

In 1881 the Swan lamp was used to light the Savoy Theatre in London.

In 1974 Mawson Swan & Morgan was taken over by Midland Educational Co Ltd and it finally ceased trading in 1986.

In 1987 Mawson & Proctor ceased trading under that name having been taken over by AAH Holdings PLC.

The Artistic Richardsons

George was born the eldest son of Thomas Richardson and Dorothy Ridley and Dorothy of course was a daughter of the Ridley family of Willymoteswick and so related to the English martyr Sir Nicholas Ridley.

Unfortunately, George was apparently to disappoint both his parents and the Ridleys.

He was born in Simonburn on 3rd September 1749

Name:	George Richardson
Gender:	Male
Baptism Date:	3 Sep 1749
Baptism Place:	Simonburn, Northumberland, England
Father:	Thomas Richardson
FHL Film Number:	0252551, 0252552

Instead of marrying for power and prestige George married for love and the lady concerned did not meet with his parent's approval or more likely the approval of the Ridley family

Name:	George Richardson
Gender:	Male
Marriage Date:	29 Oct 1780

Marriage Place:	Newcastle-Upon-Tyne, Northumberland, England
Spouse:	Frances Hutchinson
FHL Film Number:	207629
Reference ID:	84

You will note that they had married in Newcastle as they had to elope in order to do so. George had however secured the job of Master at Blackett's Charity school also known as St Andrews Free Grammar School.

ST. ANDREW'S CHARITY-SCHOOL.

This school was founded by Sir William Blackett, Bart. who died December 2, 1705, and left to this parish £1000; one-third of the profits of which to be appropriated to the teaching of 30 boys, one-third to binding apprentices to trades, and one third to poor householders. This legacy was never paid; but Sir William's heirs pay 6 per cent, per annum on the amount, two-thirds of which, or £40, is paid to the trustees of the school.

Sir William Blackett, the son of the founder, began, in 1719, to clothe the boys; and by will, dated August 14, 1728, made a permanent endowment for this purpose. Each scholar, at Christmas, receives a green coat and cap, a waistcoat, a pair of leather breeches, two shirts and bands, and three pair of shoes and stockings, which altogether cost above £80.

There are now 34 boys educated and clothed, three being paid for out of the interest of a legacy of £50, left by Mr. John Hewit in 1738, and one from the profits of £50, given by Aubone Surtees, Esq.

The school is governed by the vicar of Newcastle and the church-wardens of St. Andrew's parish, who, with the approbation of the heir of the founder, have the appointment of the master, whose salary is only £25 per annum. He has a free dwelling-house, and annually receives a gratuity of £5.

The school-house, for which a nominal rent is paid to the corporation, is situated behind the west end of High Friar Street, and opposite to the town-wall.

The present master is Mr. James Cook. He succeeded Mr. T. M. Richardson, who kept this school from the death of his father, who was the master many years. The boys, on going to trade, receive the same presents as those belonging to the schools before mentioned.

A stone built up in front of a house, near the bottom of the east side of Percy Street, bears the following inscription: — "This School-house was built by the voluntary Contributions of the Promoters of a Charity-school for Girls belonging to this Parish, instituted in the Year 1792."

The house, which is freehold, contains a large, airy school-room, with convenient dwelling-rooms for the mistress, &c. Adjoining is a good yard. This establishment was very spiritedly commenced by the ladies of the parish, assisted by the late Rev. N. Ellison and the Rev. William Haigh, and consisted of 40 girls, who were educated, and each supplied annually with a green gown and petticoat, two caps, tippets, aprons, shifts, and two pair of shoes and stockings; and amongst those who left school every year, the three most deserving received 40s. to purchase clothes, and a present of books.

The subscriptions having gradually fallen off, the school has dwindled down to 15 scholars. A sermon is occasionally preached for its support. Mrs. Beeney, who was chosen mistress when the school was first formed, receives a salary of £20 per annum, arising from funds amounting to £536, part of which are held by the corporation, and the remainder are vested in the navy 5 per cents. She has also the profit of the work done by the girls. They are taught Writing and Accounts by the master of the boys' school.

Sadly, George's marriage to Frances was short, she died on 16th April 1782 without having children. He married again in the November of that year to Jane Miles.

Name:	George Richardson
Gender:	Male
Marriage Date:	17 Nov 1782
Marriage Place:	Newcastle-Upon-Tyne, Northumberland, England
Spouse:	Jane Miles
FHL Film Number:	207629
Reference ID:	107

With Jane, George had several children, sadly not all of them reached adult age.

Thomas Miles Richardson was born 15th May 1784 and baptised at All Saints Church the following month. The family lived at Ballast Hill near Ouseburn.

Name: Thomas Miles Richardson

Gender: Male

Baptism Date: 20 Jun 1784

Baptism Place: All Saints, Newcastle Upon

Father: George Richardson Newcastle upon Tyne Northumberland, England

FHL Film Number: 0095007-0095009

The next son was George Richardson

Name: George Richardson

Gender: Male

Birth Date: 9 Oct 1786

Baptism Date: 21 Nov 1786

Baptism Place: St Andrew Par Reg and Nonconform, Newcastle Upon Tyne, Northumberland, England

Father:		George Richardson
FHL Number:	Film	0095010-0095013

He was baptised at St Andrews Church, sadly he died in 1799 aged on 13.

Next came the twins Aaron and Moses Richardson baptised on 13th January 1789

Name:	Aaron Richardson
Gender:	Male
Baptism Date:	13 Jan 1789
Baptism Place:	St Andrew Par Reg and nonconform, Newcastle Upon Tyne, Northumberland, England
Death Date:	20 Oct 1789
Father:	George Richardson
Mother:	Jane
FHL Film Number:	0095010-0095013

Name:	Moses Richardson
Gender:	Male
Baptism Date:	13 Jan 1789
Baptism Place:	St Andrew Par Reg and nonconform, Newcastle Upon Tyne, Northumberland, England
Death Date:	15 Oct 1789
Father:	George Richardson
Mother:	Jane
FHL Film Number:	0095010-0095013

As you will see from the above, they died within days of each other, later the same year,

Then the couple had another son named in honour of the twins; Moses Aaron Richardson

Name:	Moses Aaron Richardson
Gender:	Male
Birth Date:	8 Jul 1793
Baptism Date:	25 Aug 1793
Baptism Place:	St Andrew Par Reg and Nonconform, Newcastle

		Upon Tyne, Northumberland, England
Father:		Geo. Richardson
Mother:		Jane
FHL Number:	Film	0095010-0095013

There were therefore just two surviving sons of the marriage I intend to deal with the youngest first.

Wikipedia reports as follows: **Moses Aaron Richardson** was the youngest son of George Richardson who died in 1806 the Master of Blackett's Charity School. George Richardson came from a family of small landed proprietors in North Tyne but had offended his parents by his marriage.

Richardson began business at 5 Blackett Street as a bookseller and music and print seller, he later moved to 101, Pilgrim street and finally to 44 Grey Street adding printing to his business.

In 1818 he published by subscription 'A Collection of Armorial Bearings, Inscriptions, &c., in the Parochial Chapel of St. Andrew, Newcastle-upon-Tyne;' it was illustrated with twenty-three plates of arms and a title-page, by his brother Thomas Miles Richardson. This was followed in 1820 by a larger work, in two volumes, dealing with the church of St. Nicholas, containing fifty engravings from drawings by his brother.

In 1824 Richardson, in conjunction with James Walker, brought out 'The Armorial Bearings of the several Incorporated Companies of Newcastle-upon-Tyne, with a brief Historical Account of each Company; together with Notices of the Corpus Christi or Miracle Plays anciently performed by the Trading Societies of Newcastle-upon-Tyne.'

He published a 'Directory of Newcastle and Gateshead' for 1838. In the same year, when the British Association visited Newcastle, Richardson issued 'Richardson's Descriptive Companion' of the town and neighbourhood, with 'An Inquiry into the Origin of the Primitive Britons.' It was reissued in 1846.

In emulation of John Sykes's *Local Records*, issued in 1824 and 1833, Richardson next produced 'The Local Historian's Table Book of Remarkable Occurrences, Historical Facts, Legendary and Descriptive Ballads, &c., connected with the Counties of Newcastle-upon-Tyne, Northumberland, and Durham.' It appeared in six volumes between 1841 and 1846, illustrated by more than eight hundred woodcuts. A financial failure, it was reissued by Henry George Bohn in 1846 under the title of 'The Borderer's Table Book.'

Richardson issued in seven annual volumes, from 1847 onwards, 'Reprints of Rare Tracts and Imprints of Ancient Manuscripts chiefly illustrative of the History of the Northern Counties.' He had the assistance of Joseph Hunter and other antiquaries, and produced the volumes on fine paper, with illuminated dedications and initials.

In 1850 Richardson emigrated to Australia, and became a rate-collector at Prahran, a suburb of Melbourne. Here, on 2 August 1871, he died, and was buried in the St Kilda Cemetery.

He was married, and left a son, George Bouchier Richardson (d. 1877), who shared his father's tastes; he executed some of the woodcuts in the 'Table Book' and the 'Reprints;' lectured and wrote on local antiquities; and failing, after his father's emigration, to carry on his business with success, he followed him in 1854 to Australia. He acted for some time as librarian of the Melbourne Mechanics' Institute, but eventually became a journalist and editor of the 'Wallaroo Times.' From 1874 he taught drawing and watercolour painting at Adelaide, where he died on 28 November 1877.

I have a little bit more about this son:

Name
George Richardson

Also known as George Boucher Richardson

Gender
Male

Roles

- *Artist (Printmaker)*
- *Artist (Painter)*
- *Artist (Draughtsman)*

Other Occupation

- *Sub-editor (Sub-editor Newspapers at Ballarat and Maryborough, Vic.)*
- *Librarian (ANZSIC code: 6010) (Librarian Melbourne Mechanics Institute, Melbourne, Vic.)*
- *Proof-reader (Proof-reader the Age, Melbourne, Vic.)*
- *Lecturer (ANZSIC code: 8102) (Lecturer Gateshead Mechanics Institute and, later, at the Newcastle Literary and Philosophical Society, UK.)*
- *Publisher (ANZSIC code: J)*

- *Editor (ANZSIC code: 5412) (Editor Wallaroo Times at Wallaroo, SA.)*
- *Writer (ANZSIC code: 9002)*

Birth date
26 October 1822

Birth place
Newcastle-upon-Tyne, England, UK

Death date
28 November 1877

Death place
Adelaide, SA

Burial place
Buried in pauper's grave, Adelaide, SA.

Active Period
- *c.1840 - c.1876*

Arrival
- *19 August 1854 (Arrived at Port Melbourne on the 'Great Britain'.)*

Residence
- *Melbourne, Vic.*
- *Ballarat, Vic.*
- *1875 - 1877 Adelaide, SA*
- *1874 - 1875 Wallaroo, SA*
- *1854 - 1874 Maryborough, Vic.*
- *1850 - 1854 West Clayton Street, Newcastle-upon-Tyne, England, UK*

- c.1840 - c.1849 44 Grey Street, Newcastle-upon-Tyne, England, UK

Languages
- English

Initial Record Data Source
- *The Dictionary of Australian Artists: painters, sketchers, photographers and engravers to 1870*

Next, we look at the more famous of the two

Thomas Miles Richardson the elder

He was born at Newcastle on 15 May 1784. His father, George Richardson (died 1806) was the master of St. Andrew's grammar school, Newcastle; Moses Aaron Richardson was a younger brother.

Richardson was at first apprenticed to an engraver and afterwards to a cabinet-maker, whom he left to set up in business for himself. After five years of cabinet-making, he became a teacher, and from 1806 to 1813 filled the post which his father had held at the grammar school. Then he decided to adopt an artistic career, and soon acquired a reputation as a painter of landscape. He worked chiefly in watercolour, and found most of his subjects in the scenery of the Borders and the Scottish Highlands, though in later life he went as far afield as Italy and Switzerland.

He died at Newcastle on 7 March 1848, leaving a widow and a large family, six of whom (George Richardson, Edward Richardson 1810-1874, Thomas Miles Richardson Jr.1813-1890, Henry Burdon Richardson, Charles Richardson and John Isaac Richardson) followed the father's profession.

City from Bankside about 1820

His first notable picture was a 'View of Newcastle from Gateshead Fell,' which was purchased by the Newcastle corporation.

View of Newcastle from Gateshead Fell. Held by Laing Art Gallery

In 1816 he began to illustrate with aquatints his brother's 'Collection of Armorial Bearings … in the Chapel of St. Andrew, Newcastle-upon-Tyne,' which was published in 1818, and followed in 1820 by a larger work dealing with the church of St. Nicholas, and also illustrated by Richardson. In 1833 and 1834 he was engaged on a work on the 'Castles of the English and Scottish Borders,' which he illustrated with mezzotints. These publications remained unfinished.

Richardson became well known as a contributor to London exhibitions from 1818, when he sent his first picture to the Royal Academy, and was elected a member of the New Watercolour Society. His work was represented in public galleries at South Kensington, at Dublin, and at Liverpool.

The following obituary gives a comprehensive report

Thomas Miles Richardson, senior. March 7 1848. At Newcastle-upon-Tyne, in his 64th year, Mr. Thomas Miles Richardson, landscape painter.

*He was born in that town on the 15th May, 1784; his family for many generations had been settled in the county of Northumberland, and claim to have descended from Humphrey, Lord Dacre, whose father, Sir Hugh Ridley, was cousin to Bishop Ridley "the martyr." ***

Mr. Richardson at an early age evincing a talent for drawing, his father determined to apprentice him to an engraver in the town, who, however, died before this intention was carried out.

The profession of a surgeon was next thought of, but the youth entertaining a strong aversion to it, and moreover having a mechanical turn of mind, persisted in being apprenticed to a cabinet-maker and joiner, whom he served seven years, suffering great hardships and misery during a considerable part of the time from the brutality of his master. Notwithstanding the privations he endured, and the exactions demanded of him, for like the Israelites of old he was required, not only to make bricks, but to prevent him from drawing, he still found occasional opportunities of practising his favourite pursuit.

The term of his servitude having expired, he started in business on his own account, and continued in it for five years.

In 1806, on the death of his father, who was master of St. Andrew's Grammar School at Newcastle, Mr. Richardson was appointed his successor; when all his spare time was occupied in the study of painting, but more from a love of the art than from any idea of pursuing it as a profession.

His health however began to show symptoms of an alarming character; and, his medical advisers having re commended a sea voyage, he shipped himself on board a Newcastle trader, and in due time arrived in London. Here, pas sing along the Strand one day, he saw in a shop-window a drawing by David Cox, which he very much wished to possess; but his finances would not allow him to pay the price demanded, twenty guineas; he therefore returned to the window and studied it for a full hour.

The sight of this picture determined his future career; he went back to Newcastle, his health having improved, with the fixed purpose of emulating what he so much admired.

Mr. Richardson in after years used to say, he would buy that drawing at any price could he but meet with it, it, as it was the incentive to his own subsequent success.

After practising as a drawing-master about seven years, he resigned his appointment at the school, in order to devote himself entirely to the profession he had chosen.

The first picture of any magnitude he painted was a "View of Newcastle from Gateshead Fell," which was purchased by the corporation of the town. This was followed by many other excellent works, principally landscape and marine views from the picturesque scenery in his native county and places adjoining it; many of these were exhibited at the Royal Academy and the British Institution.

He was also a member of the New Water colour Society, to which he contributed many valuable drawings. During the autumn of last year (1847) an exhibition of the works of Mr. Richardson and his sons was open at Newcastle, which showed their talent and industry in a most favourable light.

In 1816, he and the late Mr. Dixon commenced an illustrated work in aqua tint, of the Scenery about Newcastle and the northern counties; but very few numbers appeared.

In 1833 his brother, Mr. M. A. Richardson, and himself, under. took the joint publication of the "Castles of the English and Scottish Borders," a splendid work, intended to supply the defects of Scott's "Border Antiquities." This was a work got up in a superior style; the plates were in mezzotint, and engraved by him without any assistance whatever; but, in consequence of this, the delay between the periods of publication very materially reduced the subscriptions, diminished by deaths, removals, and otherwise, so that after two numbers had appeared and a third also nearly completed, the work was relinquished.

A few years previous he had etched, and, in conjunction with his brother, published, a series of etchings of antiquities in Newcastle-upon-Tyne, many of which are now levelled with the ground;

and at different times engraved his large views of Melrose and Dryburgh Abbeys, as also by the aid of a private lithographic press, produced various prints of the "Side, Newcastle," "Easby Abbey on the Swale," "Alnwick

Bridge," and several other subjects of great excellence, both as regards design and manipulation.

After devoting nearly thirty-six years of his life to the practice of the arts, his constitution, never robust, began to give way, and on the 7th of March he breathed his last, leaving a widow and large family, of whom the eldest surviving is the present valuable member of the Old Water colour Society.

As a landscape painter, Mr. Richardson obtained considerable reputation, not only in his own locality but also in the metropolis. His conception was good, his execution bold, original, and true to nature. In the delineation of castles and ruins seen under the effects of sunset, he was surpassed by few; and his arrangement and treatment of aerial perspective were eminently successful. (Published in Gentleman's Magazine 1848 and copied from Art Union Journal.)

*You will note that I placed an asterisk at the end of the second paragraph of the obituary this is because the following month at the request of his nephew; George Bouchier Richardson, the Gentleman's Magazine published a clarification of his ancestry. I had referred to the amendment earlier but I repeat it below:

We have received from a nephew of the late Mr. T. M. Richardson, (whose memoir was quoted from the Art Union Journal in our last,) the following correction of an error as respects his descent.

The family to which Mr. Richardson belonged, had been seated for some generations in North Tynedale, where they possessed property in the village of Wark upon-Tyne and its vicinity.

Thomas Richardson, the grandfather of the artist, married Dorothy, daughter of Cuthbert Ridley, of Tecket, near Simonburn, in that county, a substantial yeoman, descended of that Cuthbert Ridley who was the grandson of Sir Nicholas Ridley, of Willymoteswick, by his wife Mabel, daughter of Sir Philip Dacre, of Morpeth, third son of Humphrey lord Dacre, which Sir Nicholas' father (Sir Hugh Ridley, of Willymoteswick,) was cousin to Nicholas Ridley, D.D. Bishop of London, whom Thoresby designates as "the learnedest Marian martyr."

In addition, he was pro-active in making contemporary art available to the people

At the beginning of the 19th century Newcastle upon Tyne was established as a centre of some artistic merit predominantly in the field of book illustration and printing from the workshop of Thomas Bewick. The Literary and Philosophical Society was founded in 1793 and the Society of Antiquaries in 1813.

The Industrial Revolution increased Newcastle's population and its wealth through the shipping, coal and iron industries; railways followed and engineering was developed. Visually the city underwent a change from a medieval town to one of remarkable modern elegance through the partnership of John Dobson and Richard Grainger in the 1820s.

On the 29th July 1822. a group of amateurs and professional artists met at the studio of **Thomas Miles Richardson**. *Senior at 4 Brunswick Place. Newcastle upon Tyne. In common with many groups of artists throughout the provinces they felt that*

an annual art exhibition should be held in the city and so formed The Northumberland Institution for The Promotion of The Fine Arts.

In September of that year the first exhibition was held in a small gallery in Brunswick Place. The entrance fee was a shilling, season tickets five shillings and the catalogue sixpence. Richardson was Treasurer and amongst the members of the Committee we find such well-known names as Thomas and Robert Bewick. Joseph Crawhall. John Dobson. Henry Perlee Parker and James Ramsay.

Exhibitions were held annually up to and including 1827. In 1825, the staircase was altered. According to the Tyne Mercury the staircase no longer rises through the middle of the floor .... and the light is also considerably improved. Another notable feature of the 1825 exhibition was the display of T.M. Richardson's large canvas illustrating a scene from Walter Scott's Marmion for which a descriptive pamphlet was available.

Richardson and Henry Perlee Parker decided to speculate further. They bought a plot of land on Blackett Street from Richard Grainger for £113.10s. and commissioned John Dobson to design a building suitable not only for the display of paintings but one which could be adapted to the holding of public meetings and concerts. Unknown to them, however, Grainger built a larger room nearby and called it the "Music Hall" and by doing so deprived Richardson and Perlee Parker of valuable revenue. Until its demolition in the 1960s the gallery stood almost opposite the south east corner of Eldon Square, built "ornamental polished stone front" contrasting with the other brick-built buildings in the street. Architecturally it was an unusual design, ambitious and classical, with two large Corinthian columns and recessed central bays on the first storey.

The name of the Institution was changed to the more imposing title of Northern Academy of Arts bringing it into line with the academies of London and Edinburgh. The first of the new series of exhibitions was held in June 1828 and the catalogue price was increased to one shilling; sculpture and drawings were now included and among the important exhibitors were John Linnell, Francis Danby and J.M.W. Turner. The elegance of the design and decor was noted at the time and we learn from the catalogue that there was a border of red cloth designed as a protective barrier between the public and the paintings.

Thomas Oliver's New Picture of Newcastle upon Tyne, ("A luminous guide to the stranger") of 1831, notes that "the interior of the building formed two octagonal apartments, by columns that can be removed at pleasure and also contains a room at each side of the entrance."

In the autumn of 1828, the wealthy and aristocratic patrons of the area organised an Old Masters exhibition in the Academy providing examples from their own collections. This was not a popular move with the professional artists who were annoyed at missing an opportunity to have contemporary work on sale. However, such an exhibition was an invaluable experience for any young artists anxious to further their study by copying major works of art.

Although antagonism towards the management of the Academy existed, and occasionally manifested itself in bitter exchanges of letters in the local press, this did not lessen the energies of T.M. Richardson, Senior, who was involved in late 1830 in the foundation and organisation of the Northern

Society of Painters in Watercolour. This society held its first exhibition the next year. The Northern Academy, however, was taken over by shareholders in 1831, surviving for only a further eight years. After its demise Richardson and Parker, by now no longer on good terms, were obliged to pay off the large mortgage.

In 1844 a Government School of Design was set up in Newcastle. The master appointed was William Bell Scott (1811-1890) a Scottish artist of some merit most notable for his close friendship with the Pre-Raphaelite circle, in particular Dante Gabriel Rossetti. His reminiscences in a two-volume autobiography provide us with an interesting description of Newcastle in the early 1840s: "the old Northumbrian town was then a mixture of almost medieval tenements with the newest splendidly built streets. . . this contrast of the old and new side by side was intensely interesting. There was the old market in the open air amid rain and mud, and a canvas booth and covered wagons, and here the new town. . . and the long arcades of iron and glass with walks appropriated to all classes of goods."

The new School encountered many problems, including the antagonism of Richardson. Senior who felt his livelihood and that of other drawing masters was being threatened.

However, the scheme began to improve and develop and many notable local artists studied at the Government School including Henry Hetherington Emmerson, John Surtees, Charles Napier Hemy, and Ralph Hedley.

This is another brief report of Thomas Miles Richardson senior

Thomas Miles Richardson, Senior (1784-1848)

Thomas Miles Richardson was born on Ballast Hills in the parish of All Saints, Newcastle upon Tyne, in 1784. The primary force in the artistic development of early 19th century Newcastle he is also notable as the father of the Richardson family of painters. His sons Thomas Miles Junior, Henry Burdon, Edward, Charles, George and John Isaac all became professional painters. Apprenticed to a cabinet maker he continued in that trade until 1806 when, on his father's death, he took over his job at St. Andrew's Free School and began to give private drawing lessons.

Supposedly inspired by seeing a drawing by David Cox whilst on a recuperative holiday in London, Richardson returned to Newcastle and in 1815 took up painting professionally.

His first success came in 1814 when his View of the Old Fish Market, Newcastle upon Tyne was exhibited at the Royal Academy and his reputation widened. Throughout the 1820s Richardson was involved with the foundation of various art academies in the City. To attract visitors to the Northern Academy in Blackett Street and away from Grainger's rival Music Hall, Richardson painted a series of large dramatic dioramas in 1830.

Richardson gained official recognition in 1833 when the Corporation of Newcastle upon Tyne purchased. for the sum of 50 guineas. his very large landscape view of Newcastle from Gateshead Fell.

In 1835 the view of The Side, Newcastle, procession of The High Sheriff of Northumberland Going to Meet the Judges was also purchased by the Corporation and is now in the Mansion House, Newcastle.

Richardson exhibited in London at the Royal Academy and the British Institution throughout his career but lived and worked in Newcastle until his death in 1848.

Name:	Thomas Miles Richardson
Birth Date:	1784
Birth Place:	Newcastle-upon-Tyne, Metropolitan Borough of Newcastle upon Tyne, Tyne and Wear, England
Death Date:	7 Mar 1848
Cemetery:	Old Jesmond General Cemetery
Burial or Cremation Place:	Newcastle-upon-Tyne, Metropolitan Borough of Newcastle upon Tyne, Tyne and Wear, England
Has Bio?	Y
Spouse:	Deborah Richardson
Children:	George Richardson Eliza Richardson
URL:	https://www.findagrave.com/mem...

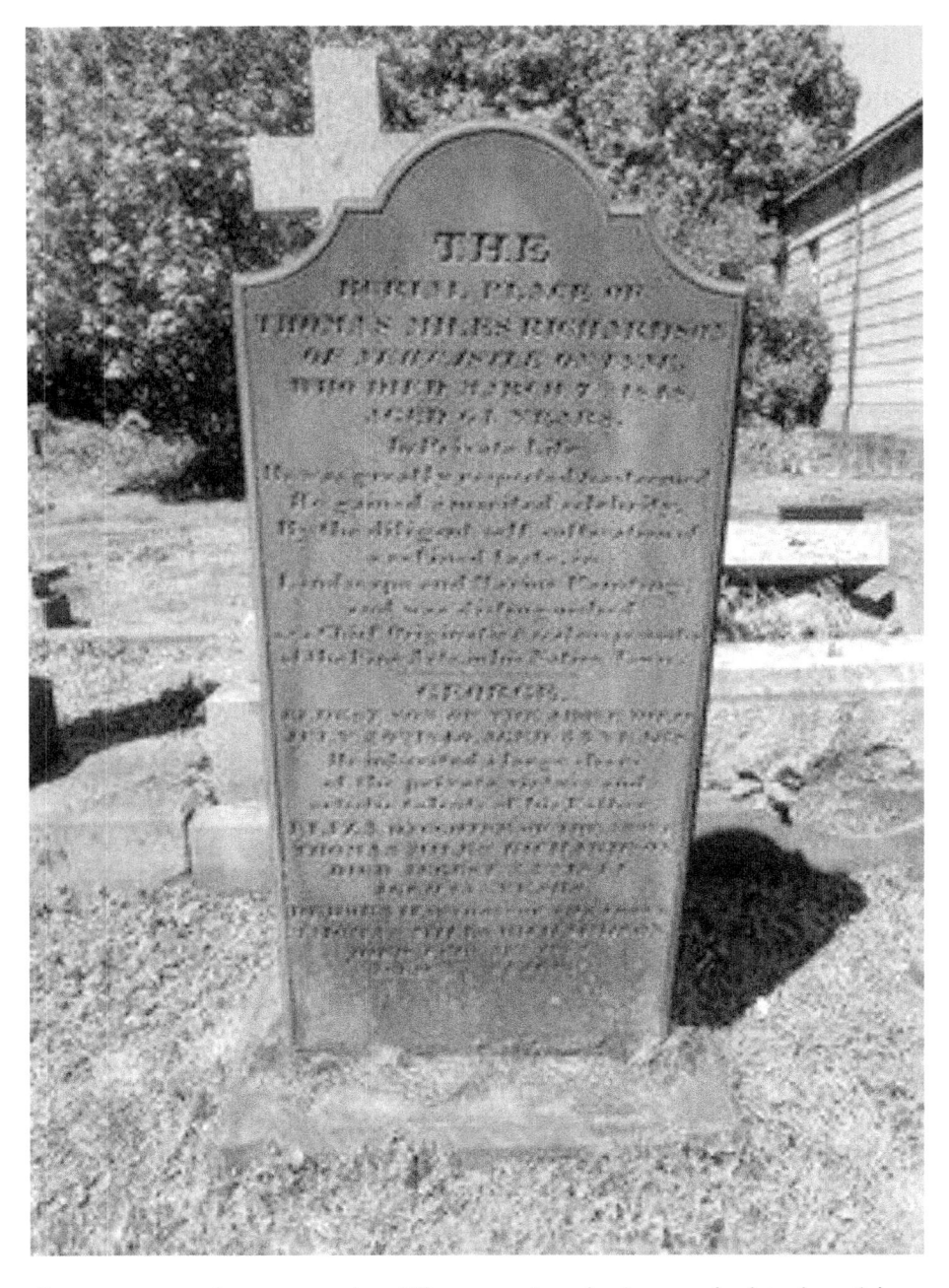

On a personal perspective Thomas (senior) married twice, his first wife, with whom he had children, was Margaret Shepherd

Name: Thomas Miles Richardson

Gender:	Male
Marriage Date:	12 Jan 1806
Marriage Place:	St. Andrew's, Newcastle-Upon-Tyne, Northumberland, England
Spouse:	Margaret Shepherd
FHL Film Number:	847923
Reference ID:	32

Their children were:

George Richardson 1807-1840

Edward Richardson 1810-1874

Thomas Miles Richardson (junior) 1813-1890

Sadly, Margaret died aged just 38 in 1823

Name:	Margt. Richardson
Gender:	Female
Age:	38
Birth Date:	1785
Burial Date:	24 Mar 1823
Burial Place:	St. John, Newcastle-Upon-Tyne, Northumberland, England
FHL Film Number:	847921

Reference ID: p 206

The following year he married again

Name:	Thomas Miles Richardson
Gender:	Male
Marriage Date:	2 Mar 1824
Marriage Place:	Gateshead, Durham, England
Spouse:	Deborah Burdon
FHL Film Number:	252794, 252795, 252796, 252797, 252798, 252799, 252800, 90786

With Deborah three more sons were born:

Henry Burdon Richardson 1826-1874

Charles Richardson 1829-1908

John Isaac Richardson 1836-1913

Leaving the most famous to last let us look at each of these brothers

John Isaac Richardson 1836-1913 seems to have specialised in animals and landscapes

Charles Richardson 1829-1908

Charles Richardson (1829 - 1908). Landscape and Seascape painter in oil and watercolour. Born in Newcastle. Son of

T.M.Richardson Snr. He practised as a professional artist and drawing master in Newcastle after receiving tuition by his father and possibly his elder brother, Henry Burdon Richardson. Exhibited extensively in Newcastle and at the Suffolk Street Gallery, London. He regularly exhibited at the Royal Academy from 1856 to 1901 showing some 28 works.

Henry Burdon Richardson 1826-1874

Born in Newcastle the son of Thomas Miles Richardson, Snr. The Richardson family were all talented artists and Henry was taught by his father and brothers. He exhibited works at Suffolk Street Gallery and RA. Gave lessons in painting and drawing. His work is held at The Laing Art Gallery, Newcastle, alongside his brothers and father, and The Shipley Gallery, Gateshead.

Edward Richardson 1810-1874

Son of Thomas Miles Richardson senior, Edward Richardson painted landscapes in watercolour much in the manner of his brother T M Richardson junior. He did not begin to exhibit until quite late in life, contributing 2 works to the Royal Academy between 1865 and 1858. 187 works to the New Watercolour Society's exhibitions following his admission as an associate in 1859.

George Richardson 1807-1840

Sadly, as George died so young little is known of him, Pigots Directory in 1834 has him working with his father Thomas and brother Thomas out of 53 Blackett Street where he is recorded as being a figure and landscape artist, His brief obituary states:

June 30th 1840, George Richardson died at his home in Brandling Place, Newcastle aged 32, He had attained a high degree of excellence in landscape painting and was rising high in fame when he was seized with a consumptive disorder and which removed him from the living.

Lastly, we come to the most famous of these brothers

Thomas Miles Richardson was a well-known English landscape painter who had reigned during the 19th century. He had used waters colours primarily as an artist and had resided in London. He had also been a member of the Old Water-Colour Society for many years.

Richardson is known to have painted landscapes, most of the Highlands of Scotland and the Continent. His works have been exhibited in different seasons and they include Loch Awe, Loch Tulla, Looking towards Glencoe, Glen Nevis, Bone Church – Isle of Wight, Via Mala, Argyllshire, Lago Maggiore and Market Boats – Lake Como.

He would use bright coloured oil and watercolour for his paintings with many white tones. The colours would also feature many luminous effects. He made his reputation mostly through the landscape as well as marine subjects.

These included the genre and coastal scenes. They reflected his fascination with the Italian and Swiss Alps. The dramatic and panoramic vistas used by him are suggestive of the Hudson River School painters in America.

Richardson had made extensive travels. He had visited the castles in Yorkshire, Westmoreland, Wales and along the Rhine river. All these travels, along with his surroundings in bucolic Cumberland, served as a source of his inspiration

Thomas Miles Richardson Jr. was born in 1813 and was the son of the Newcastle landscape painter who goes by the same name.

He was trained quite successfully by his father because he arguably became more successful than him. His career began in his native Newcastle, with his first work being exhibited at the age of fourteen.

His watercolour landscapes were achieving much acclaimed critical and commercial success by the 1830s. By this time, he had been sending his work for exhibition at the British Institution and the Royal Academy in London.

Miles had published a large folio of twenty-six plates in 1838 entitled as 'Sketches on the Continent'. It included a series of landscapes featuring France, Italy, Switzerland, Holland,

Germany among others. All these sketches were made during a tour in 1837. Eleven of these plates were lithographed by himself.

Richardson used to run a private art academy in Newcastle along with his elder brother and a fellow artist by the name of George. Being elected as an Associate of the Old Water Colour Society in 1846, he settled in London.

Richardson had become a full member of the Society by 1851. He took part in part in the exhibitions of the Society every summer and winter, thus exhibiting over seven hundred watercolour paintings until his death.

He had made extensive travels throughout Scotland and the North of England. He had even travelled a lot throughout the other parts of Europe. Most of his exhibited works were made on a panoramic scale, including mostly the landscapes of the Scottish Highlands and the Borders and the Italian views.

The later years marked paintings from the Alpine scenes of France, Italy, and Switzerland. A contemporary had remarked that most of his history can be outlined from his exhibited drawings, some of which had been local views of Britain while others were foreign. They had even implied the various seasons when the artist was at home or abroad.

The works of Thomas Miles Richardson can be characterized by clever drawing. He employed workmanlike skill in the manipulation of material.
The paintings he produced were attractive through the bright contrasts of colour and the deftness of handling. These are particularly prominent in his sketches.

For instance, while he was depicting extensive moorlands, he would be extending the fields of vision laterally by using paper of widely oblong proportions.

Thomas Miles Richardson Jr died in January 1890 following a few years of retiring health. The contents of his studio were dispersed in London in June of the year at an auction at Christie.

That however is not the end of the Richardson's artistic influence in the North-East of England. James Thomas Richardson the first cousin 5 times removed of Thomas Miles Richardson senior still lives and paints in Wallsend, Tyne and Wear. His own description is as follows:

As a child of six I wanted to be an artist, but nobody in my family had artistic learning's, so I taught myself how to draw. I used to draw on anything available, under tables and even on the pavements of the street where we lived in Byker, Newcastle upon Tyne.

I left school in 1955 and studied art at the college of Art & Industrial Design on a three year N.D.D course in life drawing, design, drawing for reproduction and printing. Around this time my mother took ill and died and I was forced to leave without finishing the course, and I never painted for fifteen years. During this time I became good friends with the Queen's artist Pietro Annigoni, our friendship blossomed and he soon became my mentor, and it was because of him I resumed painting.

Through my tuition I received a commission and painted the telephone manager P.I.Docherty the next commission I received was to paint the Pipe Major Peter Lambert B.E.M. Unfortunately, I was in hospital when it was presented at Blagdon Hall by Princess Margaret in 1987. I then received a commission to paint the Lord Mayor of Newcastle upon Tyne, Arthur C Cook, where it hung in the mansion house in Jesmond for one year with paintings by my distant relations T.M Richardson and W. Richardson.

I have always loved dogs and I showed Shetland sheep dogs for years, I soon became well known among breeders for my beautiful pet portraits of various top breed dogs. I've recently painted His Royal Highnesses Prince William and Prince Harry 'The Wild Ones'. I then sent two prints to Clarence House, and I was thanked by the Prince of Wales himself with a lovely letter.

I currently have paintings in Australia, Netherlands, Portugal, France, USA and all parts of the UK.

Contact;
Email: topdog@janpa-arts.co.uk
Website: www.janpa-arts.co.uk